The Courts and the Schools

THE PROFESSIONAL EDUCATION SERIES

Walter K. Beggs, *Editor*
Dean Emeritus
Teachers College
University of Nebraska

Royce H. Knapp, *Research Editor*
Regents Professor of Education
Teachers College
University of Nebraska

The Courts and the Schools

by

RICHARD DOBBS STRAHAN

Professor of Administration and Supervision
College of Education, University of Houston
Member—Houston, Texas, and Federal Bars

PROFESSIONAL EDUCATORS PUBLICATIONS, INC.
LINCOLN, NEBRASKA

Library of Congress Catalog Card No.: 73-81501

ISBN   0-88224-012-9

Contents

Introduction

The past quarter century of American education has been one of almost constant ferment and change. It was ushered in by the baby boom which followed on the heels of World War II. While the nation was attempting to provide facilities and faculties to house and teach the unprecedented numbers of children knocking at the doors of the schoolhouses, the United States Supreme Court issued the now famous Brown decision which mandated desegregation for the nation's schools. Before the desegregation task could be completed numerous other school practices were to undergo the scrutiny of federal and state courts. Religious practices in the schools were restructured as the courts looked at First Amendment rights. It would be established that pupils had constitutional rights and that these rights were protectable even in the school environment. Teachers also joined the march to the courtroom with demands for professional negotiation and the assertion of constitutional rights. Familiar doctrines such as "in loco parentis" were discarded by many courts as no longer being appropriate legal concepts to describe pupil-school district relationships. Court orders have attacked fundamental structures such as finance laws and school district organizational patterns. Change has followed change in such rapid-fire order that the professional practitioner has hardly had time to adjust to them before another is thrust at him.

The purpose of this text is to provide the pre-service teacher with insights into many of the major problems associated with public school operation from a legal point of view. If an individual understands the logic behind a court's decision it not only makes the adjustment to change more rational but it also alleviates much of the emotional anxiety which accompanies lack of information. Such information also shapes attitudes to the degree that practices begin to fit into the mode of legal conformity. "Due process" is as much an attitude as it is a process. The person who develops a mentality which not only accepts this process, but is capable of reacting to it without consciously evaluating his actions can operate within the demands of a new school environment without excessive pressure. The individual who cannot intellectualize legal doctrines will continue to have difficulty. The most detailed procedure does little to protect individual rights so long as the individual who administers it is not sympathetic to the concepts which underlie it. If the reader of this treatise is, after exposure to these beginnings, able to function with a few additional insights to make his professional work more productive the book will have accomplished its purpose.

CHAPTER 1

Education and Our Common Law Heritage

Many of the notions or concepts which undergird modern American education stem from principles or relationships which were first formulated in common law. These ideas guided many of the functions of government, the political community, the rules by which society resolved its conflicts, the nature of man, and the rights which devolved upon him by natural law. When the common law tradition is supplemented by the Puritan ethic, the mold for much of what we have called education on the American frontier was shaped. The persistence of some of these concepts surprises many when the historical patterns are analyzed.

Some of the traditions of educational method, school organization, and curriculum concepts become meaningful when they are viewed with a perspective illumined by common law knowledge. This chapter is designed to provide some of those insights when the various relationships concerning family stability, family roles, parental responsibility, parental rights, and obligations to society are examined. Many educational practices, such as corporal punishment, have their root in common law family relationships. Determination of pupil residence as being that of the domicile of the father also springs from this root. Perhaps the most widely recognized doctrine for two centuries of American public school operations, "in loco parentis," stems from many of these ideas. A brief examination of the common law, common law courts, and family relationships will provide us with some background for the further understanding of court actions and their influence on American schools.

WHAT IS COMMON LAW?

Blackstone utilized a brief definition of the common law as being simply "that body of rules prescribing social conduct which was justiciable in the royal courts of England." Most legal scholars are reluctant to give a more precise definition than this. A system of courts was well developed in England by the twelfth or thirteenth century. Their jurisdiction was quite different from modern practices and was to become so cumbersome that the practices have been combined in the state courts of general jurisdiction in the United States. The literature of this period frequently speaks of royal courts, courts of the counties, ecclesiastical or church courts, baronial courts, or the court of a borough. The nature of the problem or the justice that a man sought would probably determine the court into which he might go. For example, if a man had a canon law problem or one which dealt with wills and testaments he would carry this matter to the church court. If his conflict arose over the title to land, or freehold as it was called, he was compelled to take this subject matter to the royal or king's court. Similarly, the other courts which were in existence had their areas of jurisdictional function.

In contrast to the other great judicial systems of history, the common law was an unwritten code. It had its roots deep in the feudal system of landholding and social practices. It drew its lifeblood from the fact that its rules rested upon the relationships between people who had submitted their problems to a court for settlement. The body of principles derived from such activity became known and resulted in a system of judge-made, or decisional, law. The judicial activity of this period did not have the burden or overlay of statutory law so that the notion so frequently expressed as "finding the law" takes on significant meaning. If one engages himself in legal research today, he encounters many problems of interpretation even though there are written opinions and decisions; the common law search must have been much more exhausting and fraught with frustation.

If the specialized vocabulary of the law is troublesome to you, an appreciation for the legal practitioner during this period will naturally occur. Latin was utilized during the Middle Ages for most of the formal records, particularly those kept by the church. After the Norman Conquest, French became the language of the royal household and thus that of the royal courts. The dialect that developed, Anglo-French, contained the first specialized terminology for the expression of legal phrases and concepts. Some of our present-day terminology lingers from that period and each time you see the words "plaintiff" and "defendant" you should be reminded of that heritage. As the common law developed, it gradually adopted the language of the people. Even though some specialized terms have been retained, legal arguments again have begun to move back to the conversational language of the people.

LET THE DECISION STAND!

The common law writer or theoretician made wide use of theological or philosophical ideas. He was of the opinion that the law of nature revealed the will of his Maker. Human reason was the enablement by which man was to discover the law of nature and this would continue as a process so long as it was necessary to direct the conduct of human activities. All human affairs are subject to natural law, and the compacts, leagues, or agreements between nations must be subject to it because it would be the only concept by which they would be equally bound. A common law jurist denominated "self-love" as the universal principle of action which would be the prompter to cause men to seek after and pursue the rule of right, reason, and justice.

As a body of judicial and social practice developed, foundations of the common law were established. An unwritten law of usage developed which carried with it great authority. Many writers of this period, such as Bracton, point up the problems of customary law and the stability of a few eternal principles that could not change even though the order of nature continues. It begins to be evident that encounters between the permanent and the expedient would occur and that judicial decisions would occur and that judicial decisions would be made that attempted to bridge that gap. The courts were not guided originally by bodies of judicial precedents and written codes. The law became what the judges said it was so that the common law evolved as the body of rules that the royal judges would enforce. For such a system to have life or vitality there must be some rules for a court to act upon and some agency to enforce it.

The common law system involved the application of two new combinations of circumstances, those rules of law which were derived from legal principles and from judicial precedents. The doctrine of "stare decisis," or let the decision stand, grew from the desire to attain uniformity, consistency, and certainty. In any circumstance where similar cases had arisen, these rules would be applied in a reasonable manner. The judge was not at liberty to reject them or to abandon all analogy between the previous case and that which was before him. This not only served as the basis for the determination of that case but such a decisional status developed a body of law.

This legal system was not destined to remain as simplistic as it appears. The attempt to protect individual rights guaranteed by the royal courts brought about a system of writs. A writ was an order from the king addressed to the sheriff of the county in which the cause of action arose, or where the defendant lived, commanding the sheriff to bring the party accused of some wrong to appear in the king's court to give answer to the complaint. Each writ was based upon some principle of law and contained sufficient facts to bring the case within the principle of law which was invoked. As time passed, each writ gained a name, and the number of such writs increased from about 39 to more than 470 in a period of about one hundred years. Where several writs were grounded in the same principle, they were grouped. As these writs multipled, a Registry of Writs developed from which the royal judges drew the common law of the period.

The judges of the royal courts commanded a great deal of respect as legal experts exercising the king's authority and duty to administer justice in all causes. One of the leading figures of the period was a judge by the name of Bracton. In his work called the *Note Book* he had gained custody of the royal plea rolls and compiled about two thousand cases to illustrate the best in legal practice. The principle laid down in his work was that if a case was brought to the court where anything analogous had happened, that case should be adjudicated in the same manner. The use of case law in this manner was more closely akin to reference material than as a legal precedent. Bracton was an unusual scholar for his time in the sense that he was willing to use decided cases as a point of reference.

The modern doctrine of "stare decisis" varies a great deal from these early efforts to produce a legal science. Where case reporting was greatly restricted it would be difficult for such a practice to develop. In today's scheme of jurisprudence the authority of a higher court has a binding effect on a lower court in the same jurisdiction where these higher courts are those of published record. Sophisticated publishers or governmental agencies now report on every case decided in a federal court or appellate jurisdictions in state courts. On a matter of "first impression" these reports become highly significant in terms of arriving at an opinion as to how some future court will rule on the same or similar subject matter and factual situations.

Although legislative enactments and the ruling of administrative agencies play an increasingly important role in the daily lives of our citizens, they have not crowded out the interpretive function of the judiciary. Judicial decision making still carries the impact of the early common law period and there still is a research problem in connection with "finding the law."

COMMON LAW CONCEPTS AND THE FAMILY

Throughout the formative or creative period of common law development it was nourished by philosophy, both classical and Christian, as well as by theology. Those who were masters and students at the Inns of Court, the law schools of the time, and those who were renowned as lawyers and judges, formulated concepts of the individual and the family that have had a dramatic impact on today's society and social practices. According to these precepts every man was a reasonable man. Because of this nature of being able to reason, a man is basically free. Freedom was said to be rooted in reason. Perhaps the greatest achievement of the common law was thus slowly to evolve a social and political system based upon the dignity of the individual and an autonomy based upon his intellectual and moral integrity. At no point of the human condition was this philosophy more evident than in the family unit.

The polemics of common law theorists always included the concept that an individual functions at three levels: the individual good, the good of the family, and the political or social good. In each of these areas of function there were desirable ends to be attained. The common law notion emphasized the family role more than did the utopian philosophers, who saw only the individual and the collective entities of society. It was the family unit or group that was recognized at once as the natural unit in society and the strength of both church and government rested upon it. Marriage and family life were declared to be the very foundations of society and the married state was to be protected against all molestation or disturbance. This tranquility and stability was thought to be essential where the offspring of human parents were to be maintained from infancy to age twenty-one.

Certain common law principles of family relations have existed and still continue to influence much of our thought today in regard to individual responsibilities to society. The father has always been recognized as the primary representative of the family before the law. Within the homestead the father was charged with the rule of the family and the education of the children. He was given the management of assets of the family and expected to manage their affairs as a social unit. As the master of the house he had the responsibility of disciplining its members. Natural love and affection were expected to supersede formal agreements or contracts in family relationships. An old Latin phrase, *imperium in imperio,* a domain within a kingdom or domain, was often reinforced by the idea that a man's home was a domain into which the King's Writs did not run, and to which his officers did not seek to be admitted.

The father had a right to the custody, care, and education of his children. He was expected to act as a careful and affectionate parent in providing the guidance and shelter necessary for their well-being. Their religious training and personal discipline were his responsibilities as well. Only in extreme cases would the state interfere with the discretion or judgment of the father in exercising the natural role and power granted to him by nature as the child's progenitor. The common law courts were most reluctant to interfere with this natural authority because they were troubled with the idea that by such intervention a greater injury might be occasioned by their action to both the child and society at large.

One must only examine briefly the relationships that exist in today's society to see how deeply into the fiber of our society these concepts penetrated. They still continue as the very warp and woof of family concept and tradition. As a part of the Puritan ethic and of the legal heritage of our society, they are likely to continue to influence legislation and practice for a lengthy period of time. Even if they are obsolescent, as some thinkers in our society declare, these centuries of influence will not quickly erode. The understanding of many concepts related to education must be viewed from this vantage point if they are to be fully comprehended.

THE FAMILY AND EDUCATION

An early jurist wrote: "the authority of the father to guide and govern the education of his child is a very sacred thing bestowed by the almighty and to be sustained to the uttermost by human law." The common law system placed the principal responsibility upon the father to decide the kind, extent, and nature of the education which his child was to receive. Indeed, he had the authority to decide whether the child should be educated at all. As thought developed in this area, education was one of the facets of individual need which was considered to be a "necessary" for which the father was charged by the law to make provision. It took its place along with food, clothing, shelter, medical care, and other provisions which were necessary for the child's well-being. These items might be extended on credit to a man's family without his direct authorization because he was obligated under the law to provide them.

The father would often take advantage of various modes of education or training other than formal schools. Guilds, with their distinctive organization, often provided the framework of educational endeavor where the father and son relation existed or that of the master and apprentice. The control of the minor, both his person and his property, was in the exclusive control of the father. He might exercise such authority himself or delegate it to another. No civil action such as trespass or for injury could be maintained between father and child. This would include suits for support or damages for ill treatment physically. The only restraint in this regard might be the penal code provision for battery or perhaps the father might be charged in the ecclesiastical courts in regard to parental duty. Girls would often be placed under contract to someone else to provide domestic service. A part of the arrangement would often be that the family for whom these services were provided would assume the obligation of some educational training as well as the learning of domestic arts.

It was not until the latter part of the nineteenth century that ideas began to change in regard to the custody of children. In two English parliamentary acts in 1866 and 1891, the mother was placed on a footing somewhat equal to that of the father. These acts enabled the court to disregard the traditional role of the parent and make provision for the custody of the child with his welfare taken into chief account. Where the child's custody was given to the mother, the responsibility to educate the child fell on her and the child's legal domicile followed that of the mother. Those legal duties of maintenance, protection, and education were then shifted to her even though the father might be forced to contribute to their cost. The cost of education is one of the factors which help to determine the amount that child support payments shall be.

Although education at some level of grade school or high school has always long been considered an element of support required of parents, controversy has arisen in the past decade as to whether the parent should provide education beyond the high school. It has become increasingly fashionable for appellate courts to order divorced parents, usually the father, to finance the child's education beyond secondary school. Among reasons cited by the court for such a position is that of classifying college as a common law "necessary."

Before the court has been willing to identify the offspring's college support within the support doctrine, the following criteria must be met: (1) the child must be a minor, (2) unemancipated, (3) in the custody of another, and (4) have sufficient aptitude for college work. Many other factors have also been made conditions for such support obligation to arise, including such things as ability to pay, social status, educational background of the parents, age of the child, and other educational opportunities afforded the child.

It is highly likely that the college support doctrine will be expanded by the courts as a prerequisite for a competitive intellectual and economic position in society regardless of the parents' marital status and the problem of court jurisdiction over children who are beyond statutory ages for continued support. In view of recent court decisions and legislative actions, it is likely that a court with a forward look would include higher education as a part of the doctrine of "necessaries" even though the child may have reached majority before achieving graduation.

THE STATE AND EDUCATION

The responsibility of parents and guardians for the education of their progeny can be traced readily in the literature of ancient civilizations. Many of the terms which have been lifted from the literary efforts of these peoples still are widely used in today's professional vocabularies. Many still refer to the study of educational method and theory as pedagogy. The Greek pedagogue was at the same time guardian and teacher or tutor. A father from the citizen household might place a young man under the supervision of the pedagogue for the remainder of his minority. The pedagogue would provide the necessary discipline, instruction, and personal guidance that the child needed to be inducted into the adult community.

The authority and role of the father in the Roman tradition was even more dominant than that of the Greek. His authority not only covered the responsibility to educate but also to control or discipline. Like an absolute despot he had the right to discipline members of his family even to the point of ordering capital punishment for them. For many centuries parents and guardians had been accustomed to the enforcement of their desires in regard to the education and discipline of their children, first by social custom or tradition and later by the courts.

In an earlier period of Anglo-Saxon history, the courts readily enforced the desires of a parent or a guardian in regard to the education of a child or ward. For example, a 1719 English case called *Tremain's Case* (1 Str. 167) was one in which the court's authority was invoked to enforce the guardian's desire for the education of his ward. It seems that the guardian wished his ward to attend Cambridge while the latter preferred to go to Oxford. By court messenger the ward was escorted to Cambridge but as soon as was possible he returned to Oxford. The court, on petition of the guardian, then ordered the ward to return to Cambridge and to be kept there to satisfy the wishes of the guardian. Such powerful prerogatives on the part of parents and guardians have gradually eroded. Such erosion has accelerated with the advent of compulsory attendance laws both in the United States and in England.

The interest of the state or sovereign in promoting the welfare of its citizens has greatly increased, and public free schools have brought about a general dissemination which many have felt is the strongest attribute of a free society. As state after state in the United States has enacted compulsory attendance laws the ability to make decisions which control the extent and nature of the education of his child has been wrenched from the parent. In all fifty states there is now a mandate announced in its statutes that a child must attend schools between certain ages, such as six to seventeen years. The parent's choice has been reduced to whether his child shall attend a public, private, or parochial school. No longer may the parent determine whether or not the child shall be educated.

The state has also assumed that it may determine to a large degree the nature of the educational program that a child may undertake by the system of required courses to be offered by an accredited school. Although the elective system provides some areas of student or parental choice, such prerogatives are limited in scope and by the availability of funds or staffing. The legal and administrative remedies available to the parent in conflict with the school authorities have been and are quite limited. Statutes and judicial decisions frequently require the complainant to overcome a legal presumption that the rule or regulation of which they complain is a reasonable rule or regulation. The area of parental concern where the courts have given the most consistent support lies in the constitutionally protected areas such as religious belief, religious practice, or conscience.

As the state has assumed many parental responsibilities in regard to a child's education, it has also clothed itself with much of parental authority. The legal doctrine which has developed in administrative theory has accomplished this by assuming "in loco parentis." Literally, this doctrine clothes the school administrator or the teacher with the role of a parent when he is administering or teaching the child in school, both as to the content of the program and the child's behavior while he pursues his schoolwork. By defining the school's function in this way, school officials did assume control of the child in much the same ways the parents have controlled him under common law doctrines.

This approach was frequently strengthened by a statutory act which conferred the right of corporal punishment on school officers or teachers by suspending the common law definition of a battery when "moderate restraint" is used to the person by individuals who stand in the relationship of teacher to scholar. It has also been cited as authority to search a student thought to have marijuana or some other contraband item in his possession. Since the "in loco parentis" doctrine has been much abused, several federal court cases have declared that it is no longer an appropriate legal description of the relationship between a college and its student clientele. Several authorities have also questioned its continued use at the public school district level. Particularly, the minority school population segments feel that it is inappropriate because of the cultural and ethnic differences between them and the image of the middle-class ethic represented by many teachers.

Another aspect of this doctrine is also widely criticized. It is the "mentality" developed by many administrators and members of boards of education as they function in an educational situation in which this concept has held sway for more than a century. The decision-making authority of these professional groups tends to intrude into those few areas that parents should continue to control as their decision-making areas. Hair length, clothing styles, and various social practices such as teen-age marriages come within the scope of attempted control. Beyond concerns related to safety or to disruption of the educational program, the rules and regulations in these areas should reflect parental decision more than that of the school administration. The trend of court cases related to school rules and regulations also indicates that parents and students are increasingly willing to challenge authoritarian or arbitrary administrative actions or policies. Judicial decisions in many of the aspects of school administration which had formerly been thought to be the operational area of the administrator have brought about far-reaching changes in administrative concepts. When the legal concepts related to pupil rights reach full maturity it is likely that "in loco parentis" will have lost most of its authority when legal theory is applied to schools.

SUMMARY

Many of the customs upon which we base the operation of the schools cannot be traced to a single source. Many of the concepts originated in such antiquity that it is impossible to follow them with documentation. Many of them have been established in ancient times as tribal or family customs. An analysis of written law can only lead a scholar back to approximately the sixth century after Christ. The word "law" that we use so freely points up the influence that various conquering civilizations have had upon our heritage, since it is a Norse word and not one from the Saxon heritage, which we might have assumed. In the modern era of our legal history, Blackstone is quoted as having said, "law may be divided, according to its source, into two kinds: 'the lex non scripta,' the unwritten or common law; and 'lex scripta,' the written or statute law." Any citizen is acutely aware of the growth of legislative activity in our society and readily recognizes that its influence becomes more pervasive as time passes. In such recognition, the student of professional education should not forget that the doctrine of "stare decisis" is still a potent one and that judge-made law will continue to carry its impact. As constitutional or other issues become the heart of conflict related to school operation, the courts must translate these justiciable issues into rules of law. These types of conflict have had dramatic impact on the public schools in the last decade and many scholars feel that the translation of such decisions into a workable theory of administration is a much needed task.

The more intangible aspects of education which are of parental concern have a way of becoming the decisional areas of the courts. Such issues as "quality education," "equal protection of the law," and "due process of law" now fill the reporter system as the decisional outcomes of recent litigation. The thrust of this new current of case law will be to change many of the modes of thought concerning the organizing and conducting of public schools.

SELECTED BIBLIOGRAPHY

Books

DEVEREUX, JOHN C. *Blackstone's Commentaries*. New York: Baker, Voorhis & Co., 1886. 392 pages. An interesting source which is organized into a presentation utilizing the question-and-answer method. The author contends that it was designed to help the student become familiar with Blackstone's Commentaries.

HOGUE, ARTHUR R. *Origins of the Common Law.* Bloomington, Ind.: Indiana University Press, 1966. 276 pages. A history of the development of the common law designed to provide insights into the spectacular growth of the system for scholars other than students of the law. Glossary and Bibliography.

O'SULLIVAN, RICHARD. *The Inheritance of the Common Law.* London: Stevens & Sons, 1950. 118 pages. This book is a series of lectures on the common law concepts dealing with four basic issues of society, that is (1) man, (2) the family, (3) the political community, and (4) law and conscience.

POUND, ROSCOE, and THEODORE F. T. PLUCKNETT. *Readings on the History and System of the Common Law.* Rochester, N.Y.: The Lawyers Cooperative Publishing Co., 1927. 731 pages. A source book on common law development for persons who possess considerable knowledge of history or law. Table of Cases and Authorities.

RADIN, MAX. *Handbook of Anglo-American Legal History.* St. Paul, Minn.: West Publishing Co., 1936. 612 pages. A thorough development of legal history of the English and American systems. It is introduced with an outline of historical developments in parallel forms and developed with textual material. Bibliography and Table of Cases.

Case

Balfour v. *Balfour*, 2 K.B. 571 (1919). A case before the Court of King's Bench which recognizes the strength of domestic ties and family interests and reiterates that there are certain areas of family relations that the court and crown should not enter.

Periodicals

"The College Support Doctrine: Expanded Protection for the Offspring of Broken Homes." *Washington University Law Quarterly,* 4:425 (Fall 1969). A thorough discussion of a college education as a necessary. Particular emphasis is given to an analysis of the ways that property settlements and appellate courts have treated college support in recent years in the United States.

CURTIS, G. F. "The Old Fields and the New Corn—Some Observations on the Common Law and Its Continued Vitality." *Washington Law Review,* 40:1 (April 1965). Pp. 1-9. The text of a lecture given by the Dean of Faculty of Law of the University of British Columbia in which he encourages the greater vitality of lawyers in the application of their expertise in case law to shaping of legislation and legal practice.

"Is a College Education Necessary?" *Mississippi Law Journal*, 31:3 (May 1960). Pp. 285-93. A student comment which examines the growth of the concept of higher education as being a duty of the father to provide funds for a college education where he is financially able in keeping with his social station.

"Parental Rights and State Education." *The Solicitor's Journal*, 111:882 (Friday, October 27, 1967). An excellent short article discussing the erosion of parental authority in England.

CHAPTER 2

Governmental Policy and Education

The American experiment with a federal republic is a somewhat unique one. In framing the United States Constitution considerable wisdom was utilized in conceiving a document which would create a viable system which would satisfy the needs of an infant nation but reserving to the sovereign states which formed it and to the people certain prerogatives. Although it has not been interpreted with a great deal of litigation, the Tenth Amendment has had tremendous influence on the development of educational organization and practice in our nation. This amendment reads:

> Powers Reserved to States or People
> The powers not delegated to the United States by the Constitution, nor prohibited by it to the States, are reserved to the States respectively, or to the people.

This amendment, along with the preceding nine, was submitted to, and proposed by, Congress on September 25, 1789, and was ratified and adoption certified on December 15, 1791. Governmental function in the educational area was by this amendment delegated to the states. The outcome of this delineation of authority has been the establishment of fifty state systems of education.

Under this approach to education the various state legislatures are said to have plenary power in educational matters. Plenary means that the state has full or complete power to legislate or create the system of education which it desires its citizens to have. Some constitutional theorists contend that such widespread power is the natural outcome of sovereign states joining in a federal union with a limited delegation of power to a central government. One of the strengths of such an approach is the emergence of legislative freedom which results. A legal theorist such as the late Justice Brandeis expressed it well when he said:

It is one of the happy incidents of the Federal system that a single courageous state may, if its citizens choose, serve as a laboratory to try novel, social, and economic experiments without risk to the rest of the country.

Early in the history of the New England states the legislatures began to exercise this authority to create programs of public education. The "Old Deluder Satan Act" passed by the Massachusetts legislature was but a harbinger of things which were to come. Although many modern educational philosophers might not agree with the philosophical or theological trappings with which this legislation was associated, it did provide an impetus for fundamental elements of public education at the elementary level. The famous *Kalamazoo Case* probably marked a more significant turning point when it authorized the provision of secondary-level education at tax expense, along with the development of professional administrators to operate such programs. Many states have now extended such educational benefits to include lower-division collegiate studies as a part of the tax-supported program of public education available to all of its students within commuting distance of their homes.

Leadership in educational affairs has now become a concern of the federal government as well as of the states. Providing quality and efficiency in educational programs at all levels, both public and private, has become an issue of national importance and much governmental policy now finds expression through this channel. The federal Congress has by its taxing and spending authority influenced in a marked fashion the emphasis placed on areas of the curriculum which it has considered to be of national interest. In one era agriculture and homemaking were the center of national interest, but in later times interest has shifted to science and mathematics, foreign languages, and centers for the study of countries and cultures, and now to career or occupational education. These shifts in policy have been dictated as much by international affairs as internal needs within the country. In each case the Congress has implemented these programs through the use of grants or special-purpose legislation. In addition to the programs mentioned, perhaps the federal Elementary and Secondary Education Act has probably influenced the patterns of public education as much as any piece of federal legislation ever written. Although the basic thrust of the act was to attempt to solve known educational problems of the children in the nation's ghettos, it also was designed to provide instructional aids and libraries. Educational innovation and improved state-level organization were also fostered under the terms of these federal grants.

It is likely that a sizable allocation of the federal budget will continue to support the educational program, with a new emphasis arising from time to time as national needs and policy dictate. Recent speeches of national leaders in education indicate that a massive infusion of funds to the area of career education is probable. The thrust of these concerns seems to be that each young person who graduates from high school should have a job entry skill, as well as qualifying for college entrance should he or she desire to go into higher education.

The plenary power of state legislatures has also been greatly influenced by court decisions which have required conformance to the federal Constitution. A state must operate its educational function within the limits established by the United States Supreme Court. Many facets of the American educational scene have been shaped in this way. In the past two decades the expression of national policy has found its way into these decisions even when judicial precedent did not seem to point to the social solutions or emphasis utilized by the Court. Some of these changes have appeared at the time to be somewhat innocuous but have shaped the thinking of the nation in regard to its educational needs and their solutions. A sampling of some of the Court decisions which have resulted in different solutions in the educational realm will give new insights into constitutional limitations upon the state's freedom to formulate either by legislative act or administrative regulation its own educational plans or policies.

SUBSTANTIVE CONTROL OF EDUCATION BY FEDERAL CONSTITUTIONAL INTERPRETATION

At the beginning of the nineteenth century a wave of interest was sweeping the country in regard to the establishment of public universities which would bear the name of the state and be wholly supported with tax funds. The first of the states to exercise this prerogative was the state of Georgia shortly after the turn of the century, in 1805. As states were developing west of the Appalachian Mountains this concept was embraced by state after state because few collegiate-level institutions were fostered by private or religious groups. As the public sentiment grew in regard to the public university in the Midwest an interest was also kindled in some of the New England states, which had long been served by institutions founded by the various religious bodies.

The status of a number of such colleges had been precarious and the states frequently used funds of a public nature to support them. One such fledgling institution found itself the benefactor of the revenues of a public ferry as one means of stabilizing its finances. In 1816 the New Hampshire legislature decided that it would cancel the charter of Dartmouth College and make it the state university. The college charter had been granted in 1769 by King George III of Great Britain and its duration was to be "forever." When the various states became independent they succeeded to the rights and obligations of such contracts. With the famous Daniel Webster as their counsel, the trustees maintained that the college charter was in the nature of a contract and could not be unilaterally abrogated. With alumnus Webster delivering one of his greatest arguments, the Supreme Court ruled that the state had "impaired the obligation of contracts forbidden in Article I, Section 10 of the Constitution." The school's seal and its records were restored to the college trustees.

The case probably established for all time the right of non-public universities to continue to exist without undue interference from the state so long as they operate within the purposes of their charter. The contributions of these institutions to the educational advancement of the nation have long vindicated the action of the Court in helping to shape the future of higher education in this manner. Some feel that such intervention in the preservation of this college charter helped to bring our concept of the free enterprise system to greater maturity.

Another famous case, *The Oregon Case* (268 U.S. 510, 1925), shaped the nature of the educational venture which would be tolerated within the state's structure of common school and secondary education. The legislature of the state of Oregon had become quite concerned over the growth of private and parochial schools within the state. An act was passed by the legislature to require all normal children to attend public schools between the ages of eight and sixteen. The act was attacked by private and parochial school authorities on the issue of deprivation of property rights under the Fourteenth Amendment and they were able to prevail.

The decision of the Supreme Court in 1925 reached far beyond the issue of whether or not these particular plaintiffs would be forced to abandon their livelihoods. The whole issue of parents' rights in regard to the education of their children was examined. The balance which was struck by the Court was that the parent could satisfy the state's compulsory attendance law by placing the child in a private or parochial school for his education as well as in a public school. The state did have the right, however, to regulate on a reasonable basis the curriculum, staffing, and other features of the school program. The state could require that the school teach certain subjects which are plainly essential to good citizenship while prohibiting those things which would be manifestly inimical to the public welfare. The net effect of this decision was to perpetuate for all time the right of the parent to have available a choice as to whether or not he should send his child to a private, parochial, or public school. A diverse program of educational services is its heritage.

The school curriculum has also been shaped by court decisions under the Fourteenth Amendment. In the period after World War I, in which the Western allies fought an intensive trench-to-trench war against the German nation, a wave of sentiment swept the country against children of resident foreigners receiving instruction in their mother tongue. It particularly expressed itself against those individuals or communities which had a German heritage. The Nebraska legislature had passed a state statute barring the teaching of German as a distinct subject in the schools below the ninth grade. A teacher in a private school was convicted of violating this statute by teaching German and subsequently the case came before the United States Supreme Court in 1923. The statute in question was invalidated as depriving the rights of modern language teachers to earn a livelihood, of pupils to gain knowledge, and of parents of the right to control the education of their children.

The Court emphasized that there was no showing of harm which the state had a right to prevent and that no emergency had arisen in which the knowledge of some language other than English would be so wrongful as to warrant prohibition of its teaching. Although the Court made a strong effort to make it clear that it was not attempting to challenge the right of the state to control the content of the curriculum of state-supported public education, nevertheless the fact remains that its power must be subject to the limitations of the federal Constitution.

PLENARY POWER AND STATE CONSTITUTIONAL LIMITATIONS

If the residual authority resident in the state and the people includes that of public education, the state constitution should probably be described as a restraining agent rather than one which grants authority. Many state constitutions do mandate certain authorities for responsibility in regard to the operation or maintenance of an efficient system of free public schools, but numerous decisions have held that the state constitution is not an exclusive source of such authority. Local school boards have been extended wide mandates of authority on the basis of delegated and implied powers. This implied authority has been particularly asserted in curriculum content and school organization.

The famous *Kalamazoo Case* is an outstanding illustration of this principle. A local taxpayer decided to challenge certain actions taken by the local school board in regard to operating a high school at tax expense. The state constitution provided a mandate only for the operation of an elementary school program and that of the state university. The Supreme Court of Michigan decided that the local board had the authority to establish and support a secondary school in the absence of any express legislative grant of power. This decision ushered in a new age in secondary education in the nation because most secondary education had been offered in private academies. Similar judicial reasoning has supported the establishment without specific mandate of many other educational programs such as kindergartens, debating, dancing, physical education, music, and others. Unsurprisingly, most of the attacks upon these programs have revolved around those which result in considerable expenditure of funds.

SCHOOLS AS AN INSTRUMENT OF SOCIAL POLICY

The public schools have become the focal point of one of the most far-reaching social changes to confront the nation since the Civil War. Racial segregation in the use of public facilities had long been a center of controversy among various segments in educational and governmental leadership. For over a half century the United States Supreme Court had announced and followed in its decisions a doctrine that "separate but equal" public facilities did not offend the guarantees of the federal Constitution. Although the original decision did not arise in an educational setting, the state legislatures in most Southern states utilized this doctrine to establish racially segregated schools. Most of the states which were involved established separate facilities for the white and black races and required attendance at these facilities by state law. A historic change in this doctrine was announced in the *Brown* v. *Board of Education* (347 U.S. 483, 1954) case. This case developed as a consolidation of four cases from Kansas, South Carolina, Virginia, and Delaware. In each of the cases minors who were blacks had attempted to enroll in local schools on a non-segregated basis. They were denied admission and were told that they must attend the schools which were segregated by race. In three of the four cases the children were denied relief in appellate courts which cited the old "separate but equal" doctrine of the Supreme Court. In the fourth case, the court recognized the previously mentioned doctrine but recognized that the schools in question were not equal and ordered the children admitted to the previously segregated school. The plaintiffs argued that segregated schools by their very nature are unequal and that they cannot be made equal, hence that the plaintiffs were being denied equal protection of the law as guaranteed by the Fourteenth Amendment.

The Court when formulating its opinion was persuaded that intangible factors must be considered when arriving at a judgment of this kind. Frequent statements appear in the decision such as: "to separate children from others of similar age and qualifications solely on the basis of their race generates a feeling of inferiority as to their status in the community in a way unlikely to ever be undone." Finally the Supreme Court said, "We believe that segregation of children in public schools solely on the basis of race, even though the physical facilities and other tangible factors may be equal, deprives minority children of equal educational opportunities." This decision has had one of the most dramatic effects of any change in judicial doctrine in this century.

A second hearing on the *Brown Case* was held in 1955. Out of this hearing came the order, directed to the lower courts, to "take such proceedings and enter such orders and decrees consistent with this opinion as are necessary and proper to admit to schools on a racially nondiscriminatory basis with all deliberate speed the parties in these cases." The *Brown Case* became the center of considerable conflict. Implementation in many communities required use of United States Marshals, units of the National Guard, court orders, and local officers. Finally, most of the states officially accepted as their responsibility the duty of setting about to desegregate their schools. Various plans were announced by local authorities as to how the desegregation was to take place. "Freedom of choice" and "zoning" became commonly known as approaches to integrate the schools. Some local school officials, assisted by state legislative action, closed their public schools and until such actions were attacked in the courts gave tuition assistance from tax funds for attendance at private or parochial schools.

Equalization of educational opportunities had been established as a high-priority goal for all of the states and many actions were to follow which would cause this constitutional ideal to begin to shape up. The United States Office of Education, Department of Health, Education, and Welfare, issued a set of guidelines and the Congress passed the Civil Rights Act of 1964. The HEW Guidelines required every school district to file plans for its local district which would bring about unitary school systems. When these Guidelines were appealed, the courts announced a new standard for approval of such plans. It was said that "the only school desegregation plan that meets constitutional standards is the one that works." Emphasis was placed upon the local school board having an affirmative duty to effectively reorganize the schools into a unitary non-racial system.

The threat of loss of federal funds and prosecution under the Civil Rights Act brought about more rapid action toward integration than had previously been achieved. The general pattern of racial representation in student bodies and faculties of each unit has been held to that of the school district as a whole. Actions taken to maintain segregated schools, whether in the nature of deannexation of territory, consolidation of districts, or splitting of districts, have been overturned where the motivation has been to attempt to maintain the status quo.

Concentrated action by the Congress and the United States Office of Education, with the support of the federal courts, brought about a very rapid change in the school situation in the seventeen states which had been under scrutiny because of their previous statutes requiring a dual system of schools. With substantial progress on this "de jure," or legally sanctioned, segregation many authorities turned their attention next to the "de facto," or segregation in fact, which is caused in many cities by housing patterns or by local school board policy. This problem does not yield itself into neat solutions. The court decisions dealing with this problem have not been uniform. Early decisions did not wish to disturb patterns of neighborhood schools where there had been no overt effort to gerrymander attendance zones or maintain attendance zones through transfer policies which kept the schools racially segregated. As white citizens have moved from the inner cities to the suburbs, they have become minority enclaves with great rapidity. As enrollments have become increasingly that of a minority race, the courts have begun to speak more commonly about racial imbalance. Arguments about whether or not the school board of a local district had an affirmative duty to provide racial balance in the school where it came about because of factors other than the arbitrary or discriminatory act of that board continue to rage.

The most significant case in the racial balance area of recent years was one which is styled *Swann* v. *Charlotte-Mecklenburg* (369 F. 2d 4, 1966) and added a new dimension to the civil rights efforts of the courts. The freedom of choice plans which had been the most widely used pattern to end segregation simply did not work. Finally some fourteen years after *Brown* the courts began to tire of solutions which were esoteric, but not workable, integration plans. The emphasis shifted in judicial thinking from "all deliberate speed" to "now." Guidelines were provided that spelled out the manner in which the courts would approve an integration plan. These solutions included: (1) *Racial quotas*. For planning purposes the school could use a district-wide black-white ratio as a guideline for desegregating all schools. (2) *Equitable considerations*. A desegregation plan may be acceptable where some school or schools remain predominantly one race. These exceptions must be justified and supported by reason and equity. (3) *Majority-to-minority transfers*. A plan recognized by early desegregation efforts which requires that the district provide space and transportation to effectuate it. (4) *Zoning*. Zoning, pairing, and grouping are all tools which can be used to foster the development of a unitary school system if they work. (5) *Bussing*. Bus transportation as a tool of desegregation is one of the remedies within the equitable powers of the courts to provide relief. In addition the Court made it plain that all of the other resources that a school district has used traditionally in its educational program must be used to accomplish a unitary system.

The Massachusetts General Court, or legislature, sought to solve the racial imbalance problem through legislative action. Utilizing a standard which had previously been announced by a federal court, the legislature passed a general statute forbidding any district to have more than 50 percent non-white students in any school. The state was empowered to enforce a finding that racial imbalance existed and must be remedied by authorizing the withdrawal of state funds for non-compliance. Where new buildings were necessary to comply with the state board of education orders, the state's participation in building costs was advanced. Intensive efforts are now underway to solve the de facto segregation problem.

Some writers have characterized this problem as city-suburb desegregation. Few of the metropolitan areas in the nation have not experienced this out-migration of the more affluent citizens which leaves the inner city to the poor and to concentrations of minority groups. Such inner-city grouping is as effective in isolating racial and ethnic minority children as had been true of statutory segregation. Recent reports indicate that segregation is now more prevalent in these areas than in the states attacked under the HEW Guidelines previously mentioned. Resolution of such problem areas has aroused tremendous opposition. Most of the solutions which have been offered are those which have immense potential for conflict.

One solution which has been offered is that of metropolitanization of school districts. The concept which is offered in this approach is that the traditional geo-political lines of school districts, cities, or counties should be ignored in shaping attendance zones which have a racial balance. This grouping has been given the name of regionalization. At the secondary level the regions could be quite large and the children would be bussed into central facilities so that cost could be minimized but facilities with the programs that are housed there maximized. The regions at the elementary level would be smaller yet larger than most attendance zones currently used with neighborhood schools. The law in this area is an evolving one, with courts wrestling with these problems in more than a dozen major cities.

The fundamental issue in this area of governmental policy is the nature of the constitutional guarantees in the equal protection clause of the Fourteenth Amendment of the United States Constitution. A statement of Robert L. Carter reflects this issue and the problems that the courts have had with it:

> Where educational policy concludes that equal education requires certain specific practices, the courts should make those practices a part of the constitutional dimensions of the equal education guarantee. Educators have simply failed to tell us what equal education connotes as educational policy, and the courts have been forced to rely on their "own" judgment concerning what the equal education guarantee requires or prohibits.

It is a widely observed phenomenon that when school authorities fail to provide sufficient safeguards for the education of children other agencies step into the void and attempt to operate in this area. These agencies seldom have the expertise necessary to accomplish the task with efficiency and economy. They repeat mistakes which were made by the educational establishment many years ago and exhaust funding without providing the progress or goals established for them. Until the preservation of constitutional rights becomes a mandate of each local school board and administrator, the direction for many programs will continue to come from the funding of special programs by the Congress or by direct court action which has become so familiar to this decade.

SELECTED BIBLIOGRAPHY

Books

ALEXANDER, KERN, RAY CORNS, and WALTER McCANN. *Public School Law, Cases and Materials*. St. Paul, Minn.: West Publishing Co., 1969. 734 pages. Two chapters of special interest in reference to this chapter are Chapter 9, "The Law and Educational Policy," and Chapter 11, "Racial Segregation and the Schools." It has interesting notes and questions in each section as well as an extensive glossary of terms at the end.

COLLINS, GEORGE J. *The Constitutional and Legal Bases for State Action in Education, 1900-1968*. Massachusetts Department of Education, 1968. 214 pages. (Multilithed.) An informal publication which has a good discussion of legal bases for school organization. An analysis of the various insights into exercise of residual powers of state government.

PETERSON, LEROY J., RICHARD A. ROSSMILLER, and MARLIN M. VOLZ. *The Law and Public School Operation*. New York: Harper & Row, 1968. 590 pages. This text has an excellent treatment of the legal framework of education covering the first chapter. There is also included a meaningful unit on the court structure for those who are unfamiliar with it.

Cases

Brown v. *Board of Education*, 347 U.S. 483 (1954). This decision found that separate schools were inherently unequal. It overturned the "separate but equal" theory on the basis of sociological and psychological notions which were not well received by many strict constructionists in constitutional law, since the decision abandoned to some degree the influence of judicial precedents.

Meyer v. *Nebraska*, 262 U.S. 390 (1923). A state legislature wrongly exercised its police power and the U.S. Supreme Court knocked down a statute forbidding the teaching of a foreign language below the ninth grade.

Pierce v. *Society of Sisters*, 268 U.S. 510 (1925). This case is known as the *Oregon Case* and probably established for all time in our history the right of private and parochial schools to exist in our system of education.

Plessy v. *Ferguson*, 163 U.S. 537 (1896). "Separate but equal" facilities doctrine arose out of this case involving transportation facilities provided for the public traveling on trains. In subsequent cases this concept was followed judicially for more than a half century.

Stuart v. *School District No. 1 of Kalamazoo,* 30 Mich. 69 (1864). The case which established the authority of a local school district to operate a secondary school program at local tax expense even though the state constitution did not provide for such a school unit.

Trustees of Dartmouth College v. *Woodward,* 17 U.S. (4 Wheat) 518 (1819). A case which established the "contract nature" of a state charter for educational institutions and recognized that state authority was subject to the "impairment of obligation of contract" clause of the U.S. Constitution.

Periodicals

CHACHKIN, NORMAN J. "Metropolitan School Desegregation: Evolving Law." *Integrated Education* (March-April 1972). Pp. 13-25. An interesting discussion of suggestions regarding utilizing a metropolitan concept for the purpose of providing racially balanced schools. Some implications of this approach on school finance are also discussed.

MEHRIGE, ROBERT R. "The Richmond School Decision." *Integrated Schools* (March-April 1972). Pp. 51-63. A federal judge discusses a decision which would require the consolidation of school districts of the city of Richmond and Henrico and Chesterville counties in an attempt to racially balance schools by use of a massive bussing program.

CHAPTER 3

State and Local Concerns in Educational Policy

The plenary power of state legislatures to enact statutes to deal with educational concerns is exercised within the limitations of the federal and state constitutional documents. The only successful avenue of challenge of state statutes is that the school practice is forbidden by either the state or federal constitutional provisions. The fact that education plays such an important role in our society has prompted numerous court cases which have been required to define its function. In addition to the ideas which have been contributed by educational theorists or philosophers, the courts have had to formulate a theory of education based upon what they deem to be the fundamental nature of our society and to insure the public welfare. It is now considered to be established policy that the state not only has the right or authority to provide an educational program for its youth but has an obligation or duty to do so. Other cases have held that it can do so at public expense and that school laws are to be liberally construed to effect a beneficial purpose. State constitutions frequently delegate to the legislature the responsibility to create an efficient system of free public schools.

THE PUBLIC SCHOOL AS A STATE INSTITUTION

The courts have long held that the maintenance of schools is a state and not a local concern. It appears that one of the fundamental concerns of the court is that a public school be classified or declared to be a state rather than a local institution. A number of courts (*Leeper* v. *State*, 53 S.W. 962, 1899), (*City of Edina* v. *School District*, 267 S.W. 112, 1924) have declared that public education is not a function of government; it is of government. Education seems to rank with other police powers such as the administration of justice, maintenance of military forces, the power to tax, or other efforts at promoting the welfare of society. The average layman is often confused when he

36

learns that the local school is a state institution and that its school board members are state officers. In fact the power that local·officials have had over schools is local management. The courts have not had difficulty in declaring that state power extends to complete control over school property and its power to tax. When property is transferred from one district to another the owner has merely designated a new trustee for its own property. Local trustees are often surprised to find that the state may require them to levy an unwanted tax or that they may be restricted by state law or regulation in other actions they may wish to take. Legislative discretion in these matters will seldom be disturbed unless it can be shown that the state has acted in some arbitrary or capricious manner.

With the advent of litigation in regard to the constitutional rights of students, such classification assisted young litigants in getting constitutional standards applied in the school environment. The prohibitions of the Fourteenth Amendment could be consistently applied if the local school official and its school board could be found to be state officers rather than local ones. In a now famous case (*West Virginia* v. *Barnette*, 319 U.S. 624, 1943), the United States Supreme Court reversed a state board of education regulation permitting legal action against parents of children who had been dismissed for refusal to pledge allegiance to the flag, citing a need for personal protection from "creatures of the state, boards of education not excepted." A First Amendment right in the "sphere of intellect and spirit" was discovered which transcended governmental power.

While public education in every state is now deemed a public duty, it has only been recently that attendance at public schools has been recognized as a right available to every child who meets the necessary qualifications to benefit from it. Preparation of the younger generation to discharge their civic duties and thus perpetuate democratic government has been said to be a prerogative of sovereignty equivalent in priority to that of raising of troops in time of war. Thus the courts have consistently supported the establishment of schools as an exercise of the police power of the state.

DELEGATION OF LEGISLATIVE AUTHORITY OVER EDUCATION

Among the responsibilities of state legislatures is that of organizing the state for the everyday chore of operating the schools. It is well accepted that the legislature if it chose could organize an educational program, fund it, and operate it through legislative committees. Although its efforts would begin to enter the ill-defined executive area of government, it is conceivable that such administration could occur. In ordinary practice, the legislature usually organizes the state for educational services using a system which delegates its responsibilities to a series of agencies—central, intermediate, and local—as it determines. Since the authority that the state wields over education is plenary and legislative, it does not exhaust such authority through a single use so that it may change the agencies or the duties which they perform in subsequent acts.

As all facets of government become more complex it is no longer expedient for the legislative branch to perform various tasks without jeopardizing other equally important functions. The result has been that the legislature creates various kinds of administrative agencies and grants certain executive, quasi-legislative, and quasi-judicial functions to them. It is a well established principle that the legislature may not delegate its legislative power, being the constitutionally established custodian of such powers, but as government becomes more complex it is difficult to distinguish between legislative and administrative powers. The question that the courts frequently use to determine the difference between such powers is, "Does the act which creates the administrative agency contain in it some reasonably clear standard by which the discretion of the agency may be governed?" In various cases these standards have been referred to as conditions, yardsticks, guidelines, rules, broad outlines, limitations, or restrictions. Where agencies have been created without such restrictions or guidelines as to how their authority is to be utilized, these legislative acts have frequently been declared an attempt to delegate legislative authority in an unconstitutional way. Delegation of an unlimited authority upon a local school board to levy, assess, and collect a tax has been treated as an unlawful delegation of legislative authority. Numerous cases which have created various administrative agencies dealing with the issuance of licenses or permits to operate certain businesses have also been held void where unlimited discretion has been vested in the agency. The result has been that state legislatures have created administrative agencies which handle the administration of public education with somewhat elaborate educational codes to guide the use of their discretion in dealing with educational problems.

THE CENTRAL EDUCATION AGENCIES

Each of the fifty states has created a central education agency to provide administrative leadership for the public schools within that state. A large majority of the states are using as a pattern for organization one which includes a state board of education and a state department of education. The trend is to delegate the policy-making and quasi-judicial authority to the state board and the executive powers for educational administration to the state department of education. The typical central education agency is composed of a state board of education, a chief state school officer, and the necessary staff to carry out the state's educational enterprise. The mode of organization and the means of appointing or electing various officers is quite varied. To determine the method used in a particular state one should consult the educational code of that state.

The role of the chief school officer is one of increasing importance. He usually will have the title of state superintendent of schools or state commissioner of education. His role, with the assistance of the many specialists employed by the department, is to provide the leadership for the state's program of education. Along with the general executive duties, he also serves as the chief budget officer and as an appellate officer with considerable authority on appeals from local school districts. In states such as New York or New Jersey frequent appeals utilize his judicial function, and his decisions are published with a view to providing additional insights into the rules and regulations which are adopted by their respective state school boards.

Conflict occasionally arises over relations between the powers which the state commissioner of education exercises and those which belong to the state board of education. It appears when the chief public school officer is elected by the voters as contrasted to the choice of the chief administrator by the state board of education or the governor. In an Oregon case (*State Board of Education* v. *Fasold*, 445 P. 2d 489, 1968), the courts had to resolve the relationships which were to be exercised in making regulations for control of public schools within that state. The state board of education wished to raise class loads under the state's finance law. The state superintendent contended that because of the fact that he was a constitutional officer that the authority for establishing such ratios should be delegated to him, not to the appointed board. The court disagreed and announced what is now the commonly accepted pattern. The state legislature can create boards of education and confer upon them the authority to enact rules and regulations for the operation of the state school system and to charge the state superintendent of instruction as chief executive officer with enforcing them.

A large volume of litigation has also arisen over the extent of the administrative authority granted under laws which are increasingly general. Frequent cases test the broad grants of authority which are now necessary for the operation of the school system of a state. Most state statutes grant wide powers of general supervision and control. Whether some specific power is within that general grant of authority must be decided by proper presentation of a justiciable controversy to the courts. Where litigation arises there are several legal hurdles to overcome. One of the most common of these is that, where a board acts within its authority, the presumption is that any rule which it makes is a reasonable rule. One of the primary burdens of the plaintiff in this type of case is to overcome that presumption. There must be a showing of capriciousness or arbitrariness before the courts will intervene in the use of administrative discretion.

The enforcement of administrative powers is brought about through various penalties or sanctions which the state agency may wield in regard to the local school board, its financial support, or the professional status of its staff. The most powerful weapon in this area is that of withholding of state funds. In the financial systems of most states the funding for the local school district is a joint effort of the local district and the state. If the state funds are withheld the district could not continue to operate for long periods. The threatened loss of accreditation is another enforcement tool. Graduates from an unaccredited school have difficulty gaining college entrance and other privileges which are available to those who graduate from an accredited school. In some cases the state board of education is empowered to remove local board members from office where there is some indication of malfeasance in office. Where local board members are elected there must be substantial proof that the dereliction of duty has been serious in nature.

The state commissioners of education and the state boards of education also exercise functions which are judicial in character. Many of the disputes which arise in an educational setting will be heard and settled before these officers. Typical of state statutes providing this route of appeals is this section from Texas statutes:

Texas Education Code
Section 21.215 Appeals
(b) . . . the teacher affected by such order, after filing notice of appeal with the board of trustees, may appeal to the commissioner by mailing a copy of the notice of appeal to the commissioner within 15 days after written notice of the action taken by the board of education has been given to the teacher.
(c) Either party to an appeal to the commissioner shall have the right to appeal from his decision to the State Board of Education, according to the procedures prescribed by the State

Board of Education. The decision of the State Board of Education shall be final on all questions of fact, but shall be subject to appeal to the district court of any county in which such school district or portion thereof lies, if the decision of the State Board:

    (1). is not supported in the record by substantial evidence;

    (2). is arbitrary or capricious; or

    (3). is in error in the application of existing law to the facts of the case.

    (d) Trial procedure in the district court shall be the same as that accorded other civil cases on the docket of said court, with the decision of the trial court to be subject to the same rights of appeal under the Texas Rules of Civil Procedure as is accorded other civil cases so tried.

This segment of the code provides the method of appeal of a teacher who has had a contract terminated in violation of his or her rights under the continuing contract law for teachers. Not all controversies are tried in this manner because in some other circumstances original jurisdiction may also reside in a court of law. In most cases the courts will require that the individual who is involved in these disputes exhaust administrative remedies before bringing his cause of action to the courts. The judiciary is coming to the conclusion that they are not equipped with sufficient expertise to correct discretionary acts of educational agencies in educating children but they do affirm the fact that they are always available to correct arbitrary, capricious, unreasonable, or fraudulent action taken by an administrative official or board.

THE CHIEF STATE SCHOOL OFFICER

The state board of education has as one of its chief functions the making of rules and regulations for the operation of the public schools of the state. These rules and regulations may cover a very broad area of operation, since a great deal of discretionary authority is delegated to them. Once the board acts and establishes its policies and regulations, the chief school officer has the responsibility of translating these policies into everyday working relationships which are regarded as administrative policy. He is charged with providing the leadership function for the professional staff of the state and participates widely in the quasi-judicial or decision-making structures of the state central education agency. He may make decisions on school finance or budget matters which have a tremendous impact on a local district. He may also exercise strong influence in areas such as accreditation or curriculum design. In short, he fills a very important role in the state's educational program.

As the responsibility of the chief state school officer increases he is exposed to frequent legal challenges to his authority or the exercise of his discretion. In a recent New York case for illustration, *The Matter of Gordon J. DeHond* (65 Misc. 2d 526, 1971), the petitioner sought to have the court prohibit the state commissioner of education from examining his right to sit as a state board member on an appeal to him and to have the state law requiring three years residency within the state as a prerequisite to board membership to be declared unconstitutional. Under the New York law the commissioner is given broad jurisdiction to review educational matters and the court held that, since the petitioner had taken his seat on the school board and was performing duties of his office, his eligibility for membership was a matter subject to the commissioner's jurisdiction. Other matters which come before him on appeal are status of professional staff under tenure laws, appropriate salary standards under state codes, and reviews of disciplinary actions of local boards toward professional staff and students. This list is by no means exhaustive but merely illustrative of the breadth of his judicial functions. As the nation has become more urbanized the incidence of litigation in regard to school disagreements continues to multiply and most state central education agencies have a permanent staff of attorneys to assist and advise the commissioner or state school superintendent.

INTERMEDIATE-LEVEL EDUCATIONAL AGENCIES

A great variation exists in the type and nature of intermediate-level agencies utilized in assisting the central education agency in carrying out its mandate to organize and administer a program of public schools. In the state of Texas a system of Regional Education Service Centers is a part of the administrative structure. The state is divided into twenty service areas, and the centers that have been established under the Texas Education Code, Sections 1132-1133, provide planning, educational media materials, data processing, and other cooperative educational services. These units appear to be service units which seldom enter into the direct relationships between the central education agency and other local units of the school structure.

A more typical structure utilized at the intermediate level is that of county school districts with a county board of education and a county school superintendent. Their jurisdiction is usually defined by the geographical unit covered by a county. In cases where all of the local school units have been consolidated into a county-wide unit, the local school board may fulfill the functions of the county board in addition to its usual functions. County boards of education in the majority of states are regarded as state officers although engaged as agents of the county in carrying out an educational function. In some states these boards are provided by the state constitution but in the majority of instances they are created by the legislature. Earlier in the history of the public school movement these offices were powerful and exercised a very significant role in school operation. The improvement of communication in establishing direct lines of control from the central education agency to local independent school district has reduced the role of the county board. Before certification was centralized at the state level, many states had a provision whereby teaching certificates could be issued by a county school superintendent on successful completion of an examination which he administered. The particular function provided by the county-level unit will be a direct function of legislation or constitutional provisions.

The following duties are often fulfilled by county boards and their staff members: administration of transportation, administration of federal programs such as free lunch, formulation of rules for pupil transfer, approving transfer of pupils between districts, approving the consolidation of districts, approving the annexation or deannexation of property from one district to another, and sitting as a judicial body to hear appeals for both common and independent school districts on appropriate matters within their jurisdiction. The above described activities and many others are included under the statutory authority delegated to these units.

County board members serve, as do most other school trustees, without compensation other than reimbursement of expense incurred while transacting school business. Several states do provide that a small stipend can be paid for any meeting attended in lieu of expenses. Statutes of many states provide that no board may enter into a contract with a business or supplier in which a trustee has an interest. These statutes are often described as "conflict of interest" statutes and prohibit the flow of any financial benefit, either direct or indirect, to the trustees. With the exception of unlawful acts and discriminatory acts under the Civil Rights Act of 1964 and its amendments, a trustee generally does not have personal liability for exercise of his discretion in his official capacity. Courts in several states differentiate between official acts and those which may be classified as ministerial. If ministerial, the trustee may be held responsible for acts which lead to wrongful consequences.

THE COUNTY SUPERINTENDENT

The office of county school superintendent is present in the school organizational structure as both a constitutional and statutory officer. The courts have had some difficulty in classification and function of this particular office because he has been held to be a state officer, not to be a state officer, a local officer, a county officer, and an office of honorary public service where the compensation had been reduced to a level of tokenism. The more persuasive of these opinions seems to be that for classification purposes he is a state officer except for certain elective or regulatory purposes where he must meet residency requirements or qualify as an elector in order to serve. The importance of this office has declined greatly in the past decade or two. Several states have reduced its status to that of an ex officio position and have it filled on a part-time basis by some other county officer.

The powers and duties of the county superintendent are limited to those which are stipulated in the constitution or the statutes creating or defining the office. In challenges concerning the exercise of the authority of such office, the courts have consistently held that he could exercise only such powers as were specifically granted and those necessary to their exercise. Although he has great latitude in making his professional decisions, the courts will not permit him to be arbitrary or capricious in his actions. He will be expected to wield his authority in an even-handed manner. The usual standard of judgment upon his action will be whether or not he has acted on the basis of the "substantial evidence" rule. A discretionary act or decision must be based upon such evidence or he is likely to have the court reverse his decision when it is placed in litigation.

LOCAL SCHOOL UNITS

The local educational program in most communities is carried on either by a common school district (CSD) or an independent school district (ISD). Each of these types of local school districts normally operates as a creature of the state and is wholly independent in terms of its corporate powers granted to it by the statutes.

A school district is frequently referred to as a quasi-municipal corporation. It possesses by legislative delegation most of the powers possessed by other municipal corporations. It can adopt a name and maintain it in perpetuity. It can hold the title to real and personal property and sue or be sued in the courts. It may levy, assess, and collect taxes for its corporate purposes. The principal difference between the school district and municipal government is that the former is limited to performing a single governmental function, which is maintaining an educational program. The school district does not have authority such as the "police powers" of local government which enables the passage of ordinances for a variety of public welfare purposes. The rules and regulations of the local school board do have the force of law, however, as far as the function of the local schools are concerned. The fact that the school district may be coterminous with a municipality or that its trustees may be appointed by a mayor or some other local governmental leader does not affect the legal status of the school.

The common school district is generally a school unit of limited enrollment and may operate a twelve-grade program or a single elementary or secondary unit. Many of the administrative decisions of officers of the CSD are subject to direct review by the county school superintendent or county school board. Such supervisory authority would also be exercised over curriculum offerings and other academic policies. Several states require that the county board of education approve all personnel contracts, budgets, and tax rates which the common school district board would wish to implement. As means of transportation have improved, the common school districts have been reorganized and children transported to larger consolidated schools. Over the past fifty years the movement to consolidate districts has reduced the number of such districts to approximately 20 percent of their former numbers.

The most common type of local school district is the independent school district. Before a CSD can be converted into an ISD it must meet various statutory criteria in terms of enrollment, tax valuations, or staffing characteristics. When organized, the independent school district carries on most of its communications directly with the central education agency, bypassing the intermediate units. Such organizational patterns have been largely responsible for the decline in authority of the intermediate unit. The prerogatives of the board of education in the independent school district are dependent upon the statutory delegation. Most statutes allow the local independent school district wide discretion in the management of local educational programs. The school board of the ISD selects its own administrative and teaching staff; establishes its rules and regulations; determines the curriculum; adopts its budget; levies, assesses, and collects a tax; and supervises its educational program. The nature of concerns and operation of the local educational units are more completely discussed in the next chapter.

SUMMARY

The responsibility and duty of carrying out the state's mandate for an educational system are usually delegated by the state legislature to an extensive organizational structure which provides educational services for all the children of the state. The structure is commonly designed as a series of policy-making boards made up of laymen and an administrative structure made up of professional educators. The most common patterns of organization include a central education agency, intermediate school districts, and local school districts. Many court decisions have shaped the method and manner of execution of both the school boards and administrative officers. Both are restrained from using their authority in an arbitrary or capricious manner. "Ultra vires" acts, or acts outside the scope of delegated authority, will be overturned by the courts. The experiment in public education in the United States has produced a unique educational framework that appears to have worked very well in bringing the nation to its present position in economic, political, and technological achievement.

SELECTED BIBLIOGRAPHY

Books

BOLMEIR, EDWARD C. *The School in the Legal Structure.* Cincinnati: W. H. Anderson Co., 1968. 266 pages. The first four chapters of this work emphasize the relationships which exist between the federal government and the schools. Separate chapters are devoted to the executive branch, the Congress, and the federal courts and their influence on the schools.

DRURY, ROBERT L., ed. *Law and the School Superintendent.* Cincinnati: W. H. Anderson Co., 1958. 339 pages. A volume entirely devoted to the legal relationships which guide the practice of school administration in the office of superintendent at several levels. It lacks the impact of decisions of the past ten years, when federal courts have been most active.

DRURY, ROBERT L., and KENNETH C. RAY. *Principles of School Law with Cases*. New York: Appleton-Century-Crofts, 1965. 356 pages. A text which would be more suitable for the student with limited expertise in law because the authors use a style of discussion followed by illustrative cases. A concise table of cases in the front provides a quick reference table to determine if a case of special interest is utilized.

EDWARDS, NEWTON. *The Courts and the Public Schools*. Chicago: University of Chicago Press, 1958. 622 pages. An excellent discussion of the public school in legal theory is found in this standard reference work. It has recently been revised to bring several chapters up to date. The author suggests that attention be given to Chapter 2, "The School and the State."

PETERSON, LEROY J., RICHARD A. ROSSMILLER, and MARLIN M. VOLZ. *The Law and Public School Operation*. New York: Harper & Row, 1968. 590 pages. Chapter 1 provides an excellent discussion of the legal framework of public education. It is well documented and provides a good discussion for the serious student in education who has some familiarity with legal citation.

REZNY, ARTHUR A., ed. *Legal Problems of School Boards*. Cincinnati: W. H. Anderson Co., 1966. 163 pages. An outline of the law dealing with school board operation. Anyone wishing to get a rapid look at school boards will find this treatise quite valuable. Particular attention is paid to the area of school board authority in negotiating with employee groups.

CHAPTER 4

The Local Management of Schools

One of the most unique features of public education in the United States is that of local management. Although a great deal of myth has grown up about this practice, a long tradition of local management has been well established, but the legal theory which supports it is not well understood. One of the most difficult concepts for the advocate of local control to accept has been that the local school is a creature and agent of the state. The courts have not had any reluctance to speak out in this area because it has been well spelled out in constitutions, enactments of state legislatures, and court decisions that a local school district is an agency of the state to carry out its mandate. The fact that historically the need, desire, and a majority of the funds for schools have arisen from local initiative has further clouded many issues. Local leadership and ingenuity have developed the educational program but the agency exists by virtue of constitutional authority. No other governmental function has a stronger tradition of local interest and participation than the local school operation.

The tradition of lay school boards operating the local school program is a characteristic which is distinctive in the American system. Most of the educational systems in the world are highly centralized. They are characterized by structures which arise at federal or national level and provide leadership and control which extend to the local school classroom. The personnel of the boards or bureau which provides leadership functions are made up of professional educators. The historical tradition in American education, both at the public school and collegiate levels, provides that a body of local citizens function as a policy-making body to manage and provide supervisory leadership. The business of daily operation of the schools is delegated to the superintendent of schools and his staff, who are professional educators.

The local management concept which exists in our schools can only be understood by a recognition of the factors which result in a decentralized system. Although the state has the predominant role, the federal and local governmental aspects also make marked contributions. The basic responsibility for an educational system rests upon the state. It has responded by creating school districts or quasi-corporations with the specialized function of educating the young. The school district is presided over by a board of trustees made up of local citizens, who may either be elected or appointed to serve in this role. The specialized function of this board is to carry out the will of the state in regard to education as expressed by its legislature.

In local school matters the board itself functions as a legislative body which establishes rules and regulations for the local unit. The interest in education at the state and local level assumed by the federal government is a "general welfare" interest. The extent of power over the local unit exercised by the federal Congress has not been fully explored and has primarily been in the area influencing development of special interests or needs through a system of financial grants for specific purposes.

THE LOCAL SCHOOL DISTRICT

It has often been said that the primary organizational unit for education is the state. Responsibility and control for operation of educational units are placed by state constitutions in the hands of the legislature. The legislature cannot get into the direct operation of the schools so it creates subdivisions called school districts to which varying amounts of state power or sovereignty are delegated. The local school district becomes the operational unit, with varying allocations of power and responsibility for the educational enterprise.

The allocations of power in the educational system are not widely understood. The issues in this area have further been confused by a choice of language used by many in referring to schools as having local control. In legal theory the maintenance of public schools is a state and not a local undertaking. All local units of government are creatures of the state and they have no powers excepting those which are granted to them by state statute. Traditionally, partial financing and administration of local schools have been allocated to the local unit. Since the local district has no inherent powers, it must look to the state legislature for any grant of authority which it enjoys.

STATE AUTHORITY OVER LOCAL SCHOOL DISTRICTS

It is widely held that a state legislature has within its general power the right to create, alter, or dissolve school districts as it deems best for the welfare of the state. Many constitutional provisions call for an efficient system of free public schools, and school districts have been frequently altered in character or number in an attempt to meet this priority. In at least one state a court has said that the legislature may abolish all local school units and redistrict the state irrespective of the boundaries of the old districts. In *Fruit* v. *Metropolitan School District of Winchester* (172 N.E. 2d 864, 1961), the local inhabitants of a district had voted against a boundary alteration, yet the court upheld the right of the legislature to effect a consolidation of the district with another. The authority to change school district boundaries is frequently delegated to a subordinate board or agency, since it is an administrative matter. Various local prerogatives may be protected through the use of a local referendum or by the gaining of a certain number of signatures on a valid petition.

The state also maintains a great deal of control over school finances. School taxes are state taxes even though they are levied by a local authority. A local school district may be required against its consent to levy, assess, and collect taxes for school purposes. So long as the local school board exercises its authority in an appropriate manner and within limitations established by statute, no judicial remedy exists against their collection. This is generally justified as in *State* v. *Freeman* (58 P. 959, 1899), when the court announced:

> The matter of education is one of public interest which concerns all the people of the state, and is, therefore subject to the control of the legislature. . . . While education is a matter of state interest and public concern, the high school being especially beneficial to the people of the community in which it is established, the burden of maintaining it may be rightfully cast upon them. It is conceded that the legislature has full power to compel local organizations of the state to maintain common schools, and as schools of a higher grade are authorized by the constitution, no reason is seen why such organizations may not be compelled to maintain high schools.

The exercise of such authority is closely supervised in most states, and taxes which are levied for funding a bond issue may not be utilized for school operation and maintenance until such special purpose no longer exists.

THE AUTHORITY OF LOCAL SCHOOL DISTRICTS

It is worth repeating here that a local school district has no powers of its own which may be classified as inherent. The powers which it possesses are those which are granted by statute or by necessary implication. The powers which are invested in the district are those of a quasi-corporation. These have often been expressed by the courts as follows:

> It is a general and undisputed proposition of law that a municipal corporation possesses and can exercise the following powers, and no others: First, those granted in express words; second, those necessarily or fairly implied in or incident to the powers expressly granted; third, those essential to the declared objects and purposes of the corporation—not simply convenient but indispensable. Any fair or reasonable doubt concerning the existence of power is resolved by the courts against the corporation, and the power is denied. (*McGilvra* v. *School District*, 194 P. 817, 1921.)

Because of its quasi-corporation character the school district does not possess the police power of a municipality and, if considered in reference to the limited number of corporate powers it possesses, must be ranked low on that scale.

Among the powers frequently delegated to school districts are (1) the right to maintain a corporate name in perpetuity, (2) the right to hold the title to property, sell, or convey it, (3) the right to assess, levy, and collect taxes for school purposes, (4) the right to sue and be sued in a court of law, (5) the power to contract for property and services, (6) a power to regulate the curriculum, (7) a power to admit and classify pupils for instructional purposes, (8) a right to employ professional staff and determine the methods and materials to be used in instructing the youth of the district, and (9) the right of eminent domain. In connection with carrying out school functions, so long as the district's operations are carried out within the limits provided by law, the board of education may exercise wide discretion in its decision making. The attitude of the courts has been not to interfere in the matter of board discretion unless there has been some violation of a constitutional right or there is evidence of collusion, arbitrariness, or illegality.

THE SCHOOL BOARD

In much school literature the terms "school board" and "school district" are often used interchangeably. This is unfortunate because it frequently results in unnecessary confusion. The "school board" is a body of people who serve as the legal trustees of all corporate assets and responsibilities and are responsible for providing educational services to local people. The "school district" is the corporate name for a geo-political entity in which the state's educational function is carried out. The school board serves as the legislative body for the district in establishing policy for operation but also exercises the powers granted to the school district as a quasi-corporation.

The number of persons serving on a board, the manner of selection, filling of vacancies, and method of removal from office vary widely from state to state. The variations are due to the differences which result from having fifty state systems of education. The local school board is charged with carrying out the educational program established by the state. It is commonly held that board members as individuals possess no authority over the schools so that when any of the corporate powers are being exercised they must act as a body. In *Rogers* v. *Board of Education of Lewis County* (25 S.E. 2d 537, 1943), this rule is repeated:

> The board of education can only act as a board, and when the board is not in session the members, severally or jointly, have no more authority to interfere with schools or school matters than any other citizen of the county.

The assumption and exercise of authority by school boards also has many problems associated with it. The powers delegated by the state often are classified as either mandatory, directory, or permissive. The duties imposed are often described as either ministerial or discretionary. It appears that some duties may have some aspects which could be classified either way but the outcomes from such a classification are quite different so a considerable amount of litigation arises in this area.

SELECTING BOARD MEMBERS

Most of the large cities in the United States have school boards with five, seven, or nine members. The most common number of members is five. Many different kinds of organization have been tried by various state legislatures. One of the more unusual was the practice of having a school commissioner, which was utilized in St. Paul and Chattanooga. Such practice was discontinued several years ago. One state law provides for school boards made up of "not less than two nor more than seven members." The size of the board does not raise a question of legal validity so long as it is organized and operates under state law.

The patterns of selection vary greatly from state to state. Those states which provide for election of board members normally prescribe that they shall be elected in either a school trustee or municipal election. Where trustees are appointed, the mayor is usually designated as the sole appointing officer. In other illustrations of appointment, the city council may serve in this role. Occasionally, a charter prescribes that the mayor and council join in the appointments. In Delaware, Washington, D.C., and Pennsylvania provision is made for local judges to appoint members to the boards of education. Self-perpetuating school boards, while becoming a rarity, still exist in one or two of the Southern states. Many opinions exist as to the appropriate number of members. The general trend has been to reduce the number of members and to make them more representative of the wishes of the electorate.

LEGAL STATUS OF BOARD MEMBERSHIP

Home rule charters of cities often refer to school board members as "city officers." Such references tend to set off a great deal of litigation because the decisions of the majority of court jurisdictions hold that they are state officers. The determining factor in this classification tends to be their function in carrying out the state's mandate to educate children. A case styled *Whitt v. Wilson* (278 S.W. 609, 1925) makes this plain:

> Obviously the legislature, . . . referring to officers of the cities, did not have in mind members of a city board of education. For they, or rather their predecessors, known as the city school trustees, whose powers and duties were similar, have by this court been declared state officers.

Several opinions can be found where the courts have found the trustees to be municipal officers. This is especially true in dealing with statutes providing for recall of officers. Even in these cases their specialized function makes them subject to state statutes even to the point of abolition of the board entirely.

Methods of filling board vacancies are as varied as their means of selection for the office in regular succession. In most states a vacancy is filled by appointment. This appointment will more than likely be valid for the balance of the unexpired term of the retiring members. The agency empowered to fill the vacancy may be the remaining board members or the mayor of a municipal district, or the law may require the vacancy to be filled by the electorate at the next school or city election. State laws often have extensive sections on the filling of vacancies to prohibit resignations just prior to an election and giving some candidate the advantage of being the incumbent when he runs for election.

Most state statutes make provision for removal of school board members from office for malfeasance, or misfunction. The leadership roles in schools are frequently referred to as "exemplary." Failure to discharge one's duties according to law, immoral or disreputable conduct, or becoming incapable of discharging one's duties are several of the reasons advanced for removal under statutory procedures. The power to remove a board member may be resident in the state superintendent of public instruction, the remaining members of the board, or in the electorate in a recall election. A provision usually exists which requires the board member to be given proper notice of the hearing, a due-process type procedure, and a finding recorded in the minutes of the body. In a limited number of cases city municipal officers, such as the mayor, may remove school members. The question of whether or not a city officer should have jurisdiction over a state officer is quite likely to arise here, but little litigation has resulted from these arrangements because there have been few occasions where the local officer has attempted to exercise it.

SCHOOL BOARD MEETINGS

School district business can only be transacted at a meeting which meets statutory standards. In several states school board meetings are subject to "open meeting" statutes which require that the public be given legal notice of an impending meeting and that the meeting must be conducted in sessions to which the public can have admission. Executive sessions are authorized to discuss or deliberate on matters which require confidentiality but the board is expected to reconvene the public meeting before taking any action which would be binding on the district. Procedural requirements in regard to giving board members notice of the meeting, whether it is a regular or special meeting, must also be met. The person or officer authorized to call the meeting must give reasonable time for the member to respond and attend the meeting if he has such intent. The notice of a meeting, whether regular or special, should state with particularity and clarity the purpose of the meeting.

Before the board may transact business a quorum must be present. A quorum usually requires that a simple majority of the board of trustees be there. In several states there are special requirements such as having an affirmative vote of a majority of the board membership before a resolution can be passed or the board transact any business. Abstaining from voting does not invalidate a vote even though less than a quorum votes and has the legal effect of approving of the majority act.

The school board must establish its own set of policies for the operation of the schools. These guidelines when duly adopted have the force of law and several court opinions have described them as having an adhesive effect upon personnel contracts as if a part of them originally. The board will be expected by the courts to follow their own policies and numerous cases have been overturned in the personnel area where such procedures were not utilized. "Due process" readily becomes an issue when the board arbitrarily discontinues its use without following the process of amendment or repeal before a given problem arises. The board policy must also comport with statutes and with any rule or regulation imposed by the central education agency. Sound policy and procedures will greatly assist the board and its administrative staff in the operation of a school program.

In board proceedings it is difficult to keep school boards from abusing the practice of appointing committees to accomplish the work of the body. Where the work to be done is ministerial, a committee can be used to facilitate board work. It has been repeatedly held by the courts that the discretionary function of the body cannot be delegated. In *Bowles* v. *Fayetteville Graded School* (188 S.E. 615, 1936) the court explained this problem:

> The principle is a plain one, that the public powers or trusts devolved by law or charter upon the council or governing body, to be exercised by it when and in such manners it shall deem best, can not be delegated to others. This principle may not prevent the delegation of duties which are ministerial, but where the trust committed to the governing body involves the exercise of functions which partake of a judicial character, it may not be delegated.

The issue involved was whether or not the board could delegate the authority to sell school property to a committee of four with a single limitation, which was a minimum sales price. Even though the board attempted to give them "final authority" the court overturned the contract involved as being an unlawful attempt to delegate authority. Similar results have occurred where a board attempted to give a subcommittee full control over fees from athletic events, both to receive and expend them. It should be remembered that a board cannot perform its functions through its members acting individually, informally, and separately.

The relationships between boards of education and various other kinds of groups, such as citizens' committees, should also be carefully delineated when such a committee is appointed. Whether the committee is designed to function formally or informally, it is merely consultative. The form of reports submitted to the board should be that of recommendations. While a close working relationship may exist between the committee and school authorities, the board of education must take the final action, whatever the recommendations may be.

MINUTES OF SCHOOL BOARD MEETINGS

Increasing numbers of court cases look to the minutes of school board meetings to provide the facts in relation to controverted matters. Many texts which are available in school law and in educational administration stress the importance of making and preserving proper minutes of school board meetings. Although a board's methods in recording its actions may be deficient in style or technique, this does not impair their validity if they faithfully record the board's intent and action. A North Dakota case, *Pritchett* v. *County Board of School Trustees* (125 N.E. 2d 476, 1955), when passing on the sufficiency of the minutes kept by a common school district expressed it as follows:

> The members of such a board and its clerk are not experts in the field of keeping records of proceedings and that the meetings of such boards are to a large extent conducted informally. Such minutes will therefore not be given a technical construction and irregularities and informalities will be disregarded, where the minutes are sufficient to show the board's intention.

The minutes of the meetings of the board constitute the means by which the board speaks and acts. In *Lewis* v. *Board of Education* (348 S.W. 2d 921, 1961) the court indicated that board records are the only legal evidence of what was done during a board meeting. Most states have statutes which require minutes to be taken and maintained as a public record. Once adopted and signed by the appropriate board officers, the minutes are official and should be available to any citizen to scrutinize at the school administrative office, under control of a reasonable set of regulations. At a subsequent meeting the minutes may be amended to show what actually happened at the meeting. Such an amendment should reflect only corrections as to the previous meeting but not show a change of mind concerning the proceedings.

GENERAL POWERS OF SCHOOL BOARDS

The delegation of authority to local school agencies is very broad and so exists by the very nature of the enterprise. A program of educating children includes activities which are so diverse that board members are charged with tremendous responsibility. The authority of the school board can be classified under several very broad headings:

1. Those related to professional personnel.
2. Those which are related to finance, facilities, and management.
3. Those which are related to curriculum practices.
4. Those which are related to pupil personnel.
5. Those which are related to co-curricular activities.

Since related problems to many of these powers will be discussed in other chapters, only a brief discussion is appropriate here.

The power to employ professional personnel is one usually delegated by the legislature to the local school board. The conditions under which such persons may be hired is circumscribed with a considerable number of conditions. It may require that a person be a minimum age and possess an appropriate professional certificate. It may require that the prospective employee have led an exemplary life-style. The contract utilized in employing the individual is normally required to be in writing. The local district must in many states agree to pay a minimum salary for a person holding the equivalent degree and prior service as prescribed in a state salary schedule.

The power to dismiss the person is a corollary to that of employing him. It too has some limitations placed upon it to prevent it becoming an arbitrary and capricious act. The statutes frequently list the causes for which a tenure employee can be dismissed, and such a list has been held to be exhaustive of this field. The board cannot dismiss an employee for any other cause. Each state provides a means for the employee to appeal his dismissal. If in exhausting this administrative remedy he does not feel that he has been legally treated, he may then appeal to the courts. The procedures become quite long and costly so that many teachers do not feel that this provides a satisfactory remedy.

The funds and facilities managed by the local school board are in legal contemplation state funds and facilities which are held by the trustees as a trust for the state. The sections of educational codes of the various states which deal with fiscal management and control are some of the best developed. The manner in which school funds are generated, safeguarded, budgeted, and expended is covered in detail in most statutes or in the rules and regulations which are promulgated by the central education agency in each state. The transactions entered into with private parties also receive special scrutiny. Members of boards of trustees are subject to conflict-of-interest and nepotism laws.

The conflict-of-interest statute prohibits a board member from reaping a personal profit from a transaction over which he had any authority in the letting. In some states the law merely requires him to make his interest known and to refrain from voting. Either a direct or indirect interest on the part of a trustee may invalidate a contract in other states. The nepotism statutes are designed to prevent the trustee from employing certain relatives after he acquires a public office. The Texas statute, for example, requires that the employee have had two years of prior employment before the trustee's election or be more than two degrees removed if related by affinity (marriage) or three degrees by consanquinity (blood relative) before the board may give him a contract of employment. In addition to other safeguards, such as performance bonds, a public audit usually is required to insure that funds have been properly managed.

In curriculum matters the legislature determines the nature of the courses to be taught in the local school. It may do this through direct legislation requiring every school to teach various subject matter. A second means of control may be exercised by delegating this authority to the central education agency, which in return publishes a list of required subjects which may be enforced by accreditation rules or the right to participate in the state's financial benefits. Other limitations have been exercised by the state and federal courts in areas such as opening exercises using prayer or Bible reading, on campus released time, dual enrollments, and foreign language instruction. Other voluntary membership organizations such as regional accrediting associations also exert considerable influence on the curriculum. The discretion delegated to the local school board in connection with curriculum matters has been eroded to some degree. It still can exercise control over what is normally called the elective curriculum, though many activities such as art, music, choral, and band participation have now been placed on a voluntary basis and the student must appear before or after school in order to participate in them. In consultation with the professional staff, the board may still exercise wide discretion over teaching methods, materials, and academic standards.

Many of the actions taken by school boards in the past in regard to the admission, assignment, classification, and placement would not be lawful under decisions of the United States Supreme Court and the various Civil Rights Acts. So long as the policies and actions taken under such policies meet the Fourteenth Amendment standards of "equal protection" and "due process" the school board has wide discretionary powers in dealing with student personnel concerns. School districts have long exercised police powers dealing with health problems. They have been authorized to control student participation in sorority and fraternity activity during the school year. Standards may be established for participation in student government and other co-curricular activities. Decisions as to whether or not to offer adult or other special programs in the schools can be made. These are just a limited number of areas in which board discretion may be used. Many others could be listed which are not subject to control from other sources.

The co-curricular activities area has been one of considerable interest to the federal courts. Where the board has established rules of participation such as academic averages, grade-level standing in school, or the number of offices which may be held simultaneously, the courts have seldom intervened. Where standards for participation have discriminated against a class of students in an unreasonable fashion, the courts have been inclined to knock out such rules. The first cases in this area involved maintaining separate athletic conferences for white and black students. More recent cases have attacked limitation placed upon students who have married or have been divorced. Most of these rules were strengthened by the *Kissick Case* (330 S.W. 2d 708, 1959), which upheld a school rule which prohibited married students from participating in athletics. A more recent case, also from Texas, required that Soni Romans (*Romans* v. *Crenshaw*, No. 71-H-1264, D.C. So. Dist. of Tex., 1972), who was a divorcee, be admitted to membership in a drama club which had been denied her under board rules. If the current trend is indicative of the future more litigation is likely to occur in this area as parents continue to be concerned about the informal education which is gaining in prestige and importance among students.

SUMMARY

It is becoming increasingly evident that schools must have school boards that are more sophisticated than they have been in the past. As our society becomes more urban and the operation of schools more formal, the performance of officers in school management is going to be viewed by individuals who are concerned about statutory, judicial, and constitutional standards relating to school operation. The ordinary standard of "good faith" which was widely accepted among school patrons of several decades ago will not suffice where actions can be shown to be unlawful. More widespread use of specialized professional skills will probably result. It is painfully evident that school boards can no longer operate without legal counsel who are fully cognizant of school problems. In a number of circumstances a board member may subject himself to personal liability where he is a party to acts which are later discovered to be unlawful.

SELECTED BIBLIOGRAPHY

Books

BOLMEIER, EDWARD C. *The School in the Legal Structure*. Cincinnati: W. H. Anderson Co., 1968. 266 pages. Part III of this text deals exclusively with the operations of schools at the local level. Although it does not have the latest decisions in regard to school finance, the author has covered most aspects of school board authority in an authoritative fashion.

DRURY, ROBERT L., and KENNETH O. RAY. *Principles of School Law with Cases*. New York: Appleton-Century-Crofts, 1965. 365 pages. The first two chapters deal with the history and nature of local school districts and are written in a style which is easily understood. Later chapters use a legal principle and case study approach which helps a beginning student in professional education to understand court decisions.

EDWARDS, NEWTON. *The Courts and the Public Schools*. Chicago: University of Chicago Press, 1958. 622 pages. The first published authority in the school law field has many excellent discussions of school board authority and operation. The book has recently been reissued in an attempt to bring several areas up to date. It is somewhat heavy reading and suitable for more advanced students in educational administration.

HAMILTON, ROBERT R., and E. EDMUND REUTTER, JR. *Legal Aspects of School Board Operation*. New York: Bureau of Publications, Teachers College, Columbia University, 1958. 199 pages. One of the first of a series of school law publications dealing with school board authority. Although many new cases have been decided in the student and faculty relationship areas, much of the basic legal relationships are yet valid.

National Organization on Legal Problems in Education. *Critical Issues in School Law*. Topeka, Kan.: National Organization of Legal Problems in Education, 1970. 199 pages. Three timely articles presented at a N.O.L.P.E. meeting present the issues of decentralizing school districts. For more advanced students of school administration or board functions, some interesting viewpoints and principles are discussed by professors and practitioners of school administration.

NOLTE, M. CHESTER. *Guide to School Law*. West Nyack, N.Y.: Parker Publishing Co., 1969. 238 pages. This is a popular book in the school law field because it is easily read and concise. Chapter 8 deals with the powers of local boards of education and would be suitable for persons with limited experiential backgrounds in either law or education.

RENZY, ARTHUR A., ed. *Legal Problems of School Boards*. Cincinnati: W. H. Anderson Co., 1966. 163 pages. An excellent contribution to the law of school board questions. Chapters 1 and 2 particularly contribute to the smooth functioning of board operation.

Periodicals

CLARK, KENNETH B. "Our Children Can Be Educated: The MARC Proposal for Washington, D.C., Schools." *CORE* (Fall 1972). Pp. 12-16. An interesting proposal for the public schools of Washington, D.C., proposed by the Metropolitan Applied Research Center, which has as its objective the overcoming of cumulative academic retardation found among minority groups: a problem that local school boards must come to grips with in meeting educational needs of children.

DOTY, RALPH R. *Pupil Expulsion, Selected Legal Aspects and Application in Minnesota*. Duluth, Minn.: Educational Research and Development Council of Northeast Minnesota, 1968. 22 pages. A publication designed to give administrators and board members a guide in the use of school board authority to expel a student. A timely and useful informal publication.

NOLTE, M. CHESTER. "Your District's Dress Code and Why It Probably

Hasn't a Hair of a Chance in Court." *The American School Board Journal.* Vol. 159, No. 2 (August 1971). Pp. 23-26. One of a series of articles designed to introduce school boards to the hazards of defending dress and grooming codes in the courtroom. The author suggests cooperatively developed codes in which students, parents, and the school professional staff participate.

CHAPTER 5

School Administrators and School Operation

Public interest in the operation of school districts has continued at a high level for more than two decades. Critics have written numerous books and articles about the problems which daily occur in school operation. One superintendent in a major Midwestern city expressed the fact that he felt that he had administered his school from a federal courtroom because so many lawsuits had been filed against the local school district, and as the chief administrator, he had found himself in the role of having to answer many of the complaints of its patrons. The pressures on educational systems have been so great that significant changes have already occurred and more profound ones are likely to spring from current litigation regarding school finance and school organization. Attitudinal change has also been evident. Where parents were highly supportive of educational efforts in the past, school administrators often experience sharp criticism from parents and other adult groups.

SCHOOLS IN A HOSTILE ENVIRONMENT

The local school administrator is now struggling with a philosophical change as well as other manifestations of change in the school environment. Most administrators are men and women of mature years and were educated in professional schools where procedures and practices were based upon the "in loco parentis" doctrine. The change which has been brought about with the advent of decisions regarding pupil rights has largely invalidated this doctrine and has made the administrative skills of the person who clings to such doctrine obsolete. The school administrator is frequently looked upon as a representative of the "establishment" and becomes the focus for pressures of various kinds in the local environment. Students are no longer receptive to a paternalistic and authoritarian building administrator. Faculty organizations demand greater participation in the decision-making process and have been moderately successful in making themselves heard through bypassing the middle administrators through professional negotiations with the school board. Parental groups and other adults in many communities view the school as an adversary in regard to the desires and ambitions that they have for their children. School processes in regard to curriculum assignment, grouping for instruction, testing and classification, and program expenditures have become suspect. The selective effect that these practices have had in regard to students who come from economically deprived neighborhoods has caused many to question whether it should be the function of the school to determine whether or not a child should have the opportunity to enter certain fields of endeavor. Such deep and hostile feelings have been generated that school personnel are frequently assaulted by both student and non-student groups.

New tactics must be developed by the local building administrator and the school superintendent if he or she is to survive these personal, philosophical, and professional changes. The new administrator must be a new breed of professional—mentally tough, highly sensitive to need, flexible in practice, and a fiduciary in philosophy. He must be prepared to face confrontation with a realization that much of what ensues may not be directed toward him personally but toward his position, which is symbolic of the "establishment." While cultivating a sensitivity toward human problems, he must at the same time be prepared to place the problems with which he is confronted into their proper perspective without permitting his personal emotions to color his judgments. He should be prepared to modify his educational practices to attempt solutions for problems which nag at school programs. The administrative technique which offers the greatest benefit to the child as the beneficiary of the system must dominate school practice. The school administrator of the current decade will have significant problems never encountered by his counterpart of the past half century.

A NEW PROFESSION

Most of New England's fledgling schools were supervised by a committee of local citizens. They were generally citizens who had a special interest in the school either because they had children who attended or represented some religious body or perhaps had substantial economic interests which would be affected by school operation. As the schools became more sophisticated and the burden of daily operation became too heavy for the volunteer citizens' committee there gradually evolved the necessity for professional personnel to operate the school program. Professional administrators appeared first at the state level, with Horace Mann serving the state of Massachusetts as secretary to the Massachusetts State Board of Education. He assumed office in 1837 and played a major role in strengthening public education by improving school finance and establishing teachers' colleges for the training of professional staff members for the schools. Within a half century all of the other states then a part of the United States had established a similar position. As the desire grew for additional information about the schools, an intermediate level of county school superintendence was created by statute or constitutional amendment in many states.

The office of school superintendent at the local level developed from a common law status having neither statutory nor constitutional recognition. Legal precedent for naming a school superintendent comes from an early Michigan case often referred to as the *Kalamazoo Case*. This case is styled *Stuart* v. *Kalamazoo School District* (30 Mich. 69, 1874) and involved a taxpayer attempting to prevent a local school district from levying a local tax to operate a public high school and to pay the salary of the local school superintendent. The Michigan constitution authorized elementary schools and colleges but was silent on whether tax funds could be spent on secondary schools or full-time administrators. The court held that the power to name a superintendent was incident to the full control which by law the board had over the schools of the district. In legal effect he is an employee or agent of the board, while the county superintendent or chief state officer is often referred to as a state officer. This distinction is significant when someone attempts to remove the superintendent by resorting to the use of recall elections for the removal of state officers.

As an employee the relations between the local school board and the superintendent are determined by contract. In the statutes where the office is mentioned its duties are seldom stated with any degree of clarity. The assumption appears to be that each local board has a prerogative to spell out the duties expected of the office so that statutory definition or clarification is not necessary. School administrator organizations in several states have attempted to overcome this problem by drafting a recommended contract which they promote as a uniform document to be used throughout the state. In practice the local board has the authority and liberty to write a wide variety of working conditions into this contract. Numerous tenure statutes for teachers do not cover the superintendent's position unless he reverts back to teaching status. Where superintendents have been wrongfully removed, the courts usually reward money damages rather than order reinstatement, indicating that the superintendent should serve at the pleasure of the employing board. Where such rulings exist the administrative position becomes subservient to the board to such a degree that innovation without board approval or participation in experimentation without their concurrence is often grounds for removal.

THE LOCAL BUILDING ADMINISTRATOR

The urban trend of population movement has brought about the existence of large school districts. Where this has occurred the districts are frequently divided into attendance zones and a school plant is usually designed to facilitate the school program as neighborhood units. Each of these attendance units is headed by a local administrator. While these units were small a teacher who had distinguished himself was assigned the responsibility of operating the local unit. He often assumed administrative responsibilities while continuing to teach several classes. Because of his dual role he was generally referred to as the head teacher or in some cases the principal teacher. As the unit grew in size and complexity this position became a full-time one and the title which stuck was that of principal. In most situations the principal is held to be a teacher and enjoys most of the benefits afforded to teachers by statute or salary schedule.

In addition to the unit administrators and the school superintendent, modern educational programs may utilize the services of many other highly skilled persons who may not be in the direct line of administrative responsibility. They usually perform business, supervisory, psychometry, attendance enforcement, food service, data processing, and other services needed for a complex organizational function. These officers are frequently referred to as middle administrators. In small districts these positions may be used in small numbers, while in the large city school systems they may number several hundred. The operation of one of these large school units is a major management task and the superintendent needs a high order of management ability.

DELEGATION OF AUTHORITY TO OPERATE SCHOOLS

Just as it is impractical for the legislature to attempt to directly administer schools to fulfill its educational mandate, the local school board has the same kind of disabilities in regard to operating the day-to-day school program. The local school board establishes operational policies and delegates the responsibility of the direct operation of the schools to the superintendent and his professional staff. The superintendent and his staff have the responsibility of implementing board policy, which consists of devising plans for school programs and providing the professional leadership to accomplish the educational objectives laid out by the board. Theorists in educational administration insist that there should be a clear line of distinction between the policy-making function and that of the administrator in executing such announced policy. Since responsibility for the local school is in the hands of the school board, it may not abrogate its responsibility by delegating it to someone else. In fact, most state education codes stipulate that the board must always retain final determination for school policy as its sole authority.

There are a number of powers which the school board may not delegate to the professional staff. Typical of such powers is that of contracting for goods and services. As a practical matter the school board cannot take the time to conduct personal interviews with all prospective school employees. The responsibility for recruiting, selecting, and recommending prospective employees is ordinarily delegated to the superintendent or his staff. They may carry the process through to the offering of a contract, but the courts have repeatedly found no contractual relationship exists until the board itself enters into a contract either by adopting the prior acts of the administrator or by entering such action into the minutes of the school district. The authority to expel a pupil is another such power which cannot be delegated. The board often does delegate the authority to suspend a student, which is defined as a short-term disciplinary action. In a majority of states the expulsion of a student is considered to be a serious enough act that only a school board may exercise such power.

THE SUPERINTENDENT'S PORTFOLIO

Since the school administrator receives his powers and duties through the process of delegation, some note should be made of this process. In most cases the duties and powers are delegated to him by the local board, but in states where the basic school unit is a county unit his duties and powers may be set up in the educational code of the state. In a few instances his responsibilities may also be shaped by the rules and regulation of the central education agency of the state. The major factor in school operation probably rests upon the relationship between the superintendent and his board of trustees. Much of the delegation of authority is informal rather than formal and often powers are assumed by the superintendent because no definitive action in regard to a problem area has ever been taken by the board. Much of the uncertainty and confusion in this area is relieved when specific policies of school operation are adopted and organized into a formal policy handbook. Many states have now adopted statutes which require complete manning charts of all positions within a school district and stipulate that a position description must be written for each position.

An analysis of state statutes dealing with the office of superintendent of schools is not too helpful in describing the role that he plays in the development of the local educational program. The most definitive statutes are those dealing with professional certification. These statutes require that the superintendent of schools have professional training in school administration and supervision. An increasing number of states require that he have a substantial amount of training in course work specifically designed to train superintendents. Welfare items also appear in the statutes frequently. These items have to do with retirement systems, tenure, and contractual matters such as length of service or reasons for dismissal.

Specific rights which are granted to these offices are limited in number and take on the character of specific duties. Some require that all meetings of the board of trustees must be attended by the superintendent and that he serve as the secretary to the board or as its adviser in recommending policy in regard to school operation. He is commonly expected to provide professional leadership for school operation and to supervise the school staff in its daily function. Numerous compulsory attendance laws make him responsible for enforcement of school attendance either personally or by some member of his staff to whom such duty is delegated. In various state codes he is expected to evaluate personnel, serve as the chief budget officer, establish accounting procedures for protection of school funds, recommend textbooks and materials of instruction, and to provide safety checks for school buildings and equipment.

The role of the superintendent in relation to his board can readily be seen to fall into three categories: (1) as an employee, (2) as an executive officer of the district, and (3) as an adviser on educational policy. In addition to these responsibilities he must also maintain relationships with the public, parents, faculty, and students. While these roles are growing in importance his primary concern must focus upon his relationship with the board of trustees. His professional training and expertise should fit him to be the counselor to the board in the exercise of its duties. He has also been described as "chief dreamer and schemer," but one does not function very long in this role if he cannot support most of his recommendations with philosophical theory and factual data that is acceptable to his board.

THE ROLE OF THE UNIT ADMINISTRATOR

Of all the middle administrative positions, the school principal is the most common title used in school districts over the nation. Principals are the first line of administrators and have a difficult position because the role expectancies which they must fill are quite varied. When a parent comes to the school, he will insist that he see the principal. If a student misbehaves in the classroom and the teacher feels that he cannot adequately discipline the child, he is sent to the principal's office. Much of the energy of student committees is directed toward the building administrator because he is the most visible representative of the "system." At the same time the principal must attempt to answer to the needs of a faculty who are aggrieved over some problem. The principal also has the professional duty to translate the educational goals adopted by the board of education into operational programs to meet the needs of children attending his unit. When the position is evaluated in terms of role expectancy it is easy to see the reason for much of the anxiety that has surrounded it in recent years.

The position and image of the principal has eroded significantly in the last decade. Much of this appears to have come about through the mechanism of the professional negotiation process. The principal becomes the focal point of most teacher grievances because of the daily contact which occurs in the supervision of the instructional program. As a consequence many of the issues which come to the negotiation table represent the points of conflict generated through such contacts. When the negotiator representing the board of trustees finds it necessary to establish priorities in regard to settlement of teacher demands, prerogatives which seem important to the unit administrator are often bargained away or procedural provisions attach such detail as to limit the discretion of the principal severely. Some of these individuals now refer to themselves as the "keeper of the keys" and the "enforcer of the book."

The pressure from this level of conflict has spilled over into state legislatures and into the courts. Recent legislation in at least one state has deprived the principal of tenure in his position. In others, the courts have decided that the principal may gain tenure as a teacher, but not as an administrator. The professional organizations of principals have set about in several states to codify a principal's duties so that it would be a violation of law for them to be bargained away in the negotiation process. One such provision was added to the Texas Education Code (Section 16.08, Duties of School Principals) and reads as follows:

> Public school principals, who shall hold valid administrative certificates, shall be responsible for:
>
> (a) assuming administrative responsibility and instructional leadership, under the supervision of the superintendent, for discipline, and the planning, operation, supervision, and evaluation of the educational program of the attendance area in which he is assigned;
>
> (b) submitting recommendations to the superintendent concerning assignment, evaluation, promotion, and dismissal of all personnel assigned to the attendance center; and
>
> (c) performing any other duties assigned by the superintendent pursuant to school board policy.
>
> (d) Nothing herein shall be construed as a limitation on the powers, responsibilities, and obligations of the school board as now prescribed by law.

A vital leadership role for the unit administrator seems to be essential to the smooth functioning of the education program. It will require an intelligent and dynamic individual to fill the role expectations at this level. If the pressures at this level continue to build as they have in the recent past, most of the job satisfactions of such positions will be destroyed and few qualified individuals will want to take on such a task.

PERSONAL LIABILITIES OF SCHOOL ADMINISTRATORS

The school administrator has the same risk in regard to being held responsible for his or her wrongful acts as any other adult in our society. The governmental immunity doctrine which still protects the school district from tort liability in several states does not protect the administrator or teacher. Many of the tasks which are associated with the modern school are fraught with legal consequences and potential liabilities. Litigation regarding school administrators has greatly increased and recent legislation has created additional causes of action related to civil and constitutional rights. The professional training of each school administrator should contain some work in the field of educational law so that he becomes aware of the recent court decisions, administrative rulings, new statutes, or regulations of the central education agency under which he operates.

Areas of special concern to the practicing administrator are the following: (1) excessive use of force in corporal punishment, (2) negligence in professional performance, and (3) constitutional and civil rights. It would be worth a short paragraph to briefly discuss these areas. The statutes which permit corporal punishment are often called lawful battery statutes. Most of them qualify its use with a phrase such as "moderate restraint to the person shall not be a battery." When excessive force is used the administrator subjects himself to both criminal and civil assault and battery charges. When an administrator performs in a negligent manner and his carelessness results in injury to a child he may be sued in tort. His performance will be judged against that of a "reasonable prudent person in the same or similar circumstances." It will be assumed that the standard by which your performance is judged will be adjusted to reflect your age and experience as well as professional training. The administrator's negligence must be the proximate cause of the injury before any liability arises. The federal Congress has created new causes of action based upon unlawful discrimination when such actions are based upon race, religion, national origin, sex, or age. Every decision which an administrator makes in regard to his program or policy recommendations must pass the test of "equal protection" and "due process." These causes of action may be filed against the individual in either his official or individual capacities or both.

THE ADMINISTRATOR AS AN EDUCATIONAL LEADER

In modern educational theory it is widely accepted that the public schools should be governed by a lay board of education, but the actual administration of the schools should be carried out by a professionally trained superintendent and his professional staff. This development did not come automatically, but has been the developmental product of a dynamic system. As the school districts grew in size and complexity, the school committees gradually delegated more and more of the routine duties of supervision to the professional. In the second half of the nineteenth century this movement accelerated until most of the operational decisions such as recruiting and selection of teachers, modification and development of curriculum, and business administration were placed in professional hands.

It is a well established practice now for the professional administrators to exercise widespread leadership in all facets of the educational program, subject to board policy and their ongoing approval of the administrators' actions. In nearly every educational situation, not only is the administrator encouraged to provide strong educational leadership, but he is likely to jeopardize his position if he permits the procedures of his school to become outmoded or his curriculum loaded with obsolete materials. The mode of such leadership has undergone a number of changes. The more recent one has been brought about by the change in judicial philosophy in regard to the constitutional rights of teachers, and pupils. The administrative leader of today must possess a vast store of professional knowledge and know-how to group about himself a professional staff who can contribute a wide range of expertise to the program. In addition to the professional knowledge that he brings to the situation, he must have a great deal of personal sensitivity and function within a judicially established framework of operational guides. The quality of individuals practicing the art of school administration will have a tremendous influence on the nature and effectiveness of American education.

SUMMARY

The profession of school administration is a comparatively young one and has developed primarily in less than a century. Its primary progress has been made since the famous *Kalamazoo Case* in 1874. The philosophies which have guided practitioners in this field have been somewhat stable until the federal court decisions which have developed during the last decade. The old doctrine of "in loco parentis" with its possibilities of authoritarian leadership and arbitrariness has been modified to a great degree by the new doctrines of pupil and teacher rights. The mentality and method of the administrator have had to change. The process has been slow and somewhat painful. Typical of the conflict have been the lawsuits filed over personal grooming and hair length. There have been well over 100 cases dealing with this issue alone and the Federal Circuit Courts of Appeals have split badly over whether or not this right is fundamental enough to merit constitutional protection. The quality of American public education is largely dependent upon the quality of individuals who can be attracted into their role and the skill with which they practice their profession.

SELECTED BIBLIOGRAPHY

Books

DRURY, ROBERT L., ed. *Law and the School Superintendent.* Cincinnati: W. H. Anderson Co., 1958. 339 pages. This text is rapidly becoming obsolete in this fast changing field of school administration. It represents a first effort on the part of a group of educators to provide legal insights into a developing field of professional practice.

DRURY, ROBERT L., and KENNETH C. RAY. *Principles of School Law with Cases.* New York: Appleton-Century-Crofts, 1965. 356 pages. This text is unusual in style in that it contains statements of legal principles with a collection of cases from which they are drawn. In Chapter 5, "Teachers, Principals, and Superintendents," the authors treat relationships between various school officers and give several interesting insights.

HAZARD, WILLIAM R. *Education and the Law, Cases and Materials on the Public Schools.* New York: The Free Press, 1971. 480 pages. There is an interesting discussion of tort liability of teachers and schools with illustrative cases and readings in this volume on pages 405 to 448.

NOLTE, M. CHESTER. *Guide to School Law.* West Nyack, N.Y.: Parker Publishing Co., 1969. 238 pages. A recently written handbook designed to assist the beginning practitioner of school administration in understanding the legal significance of various activities in education.

PETERSON, LEROY J., RICHARD A. ROSSMILLER, and MARLIN M. VOLZ. *The Law and Public School Operation.* New York: Harper & Row, 1969. 590 pages. Chapter 10 is a well written discussion of tort liability as it relates to school districts, school officers, and school employees. A wealth of case material is available in the footnotes, which are used to document various statements.

Periodicals

KUKLA, DAVID A. "Protest in Black and White: Student Radicals in High Schools." *Bulletin.* National Association of Secondary School Principals, January 1970, Pp. 72-86. This author urges the principal to see the educational opportunity to involve the student radical in constructive activities in which the student contributes meaningfully to the educational program.

MORAN, K. DONALD. "The Doctrine of In Loco Parentis, Past and Present." *Conference Proceedings, 1967*. Topeka, Kan.: National Organization of Legal Problems in Education, 1968. No pagination. This presentation is a historical development of the doctrine of "in loco parentis." The author traces the concept of parental authority from Hammurabi to the Anglo-Saxon tradition in an attempt to provide an understanding of this concept.

SHANKS, HERSHEL. "Equal Education and the Law." *The American Scholar*. Vol. 39, No. 2 (Spring 1970). Pp. 225-69. An interesting and scholarly treatment of the development of equal protection doctrine. The author gives particular insights into suits which are pending in regard to "equal protection" arguments.

WILSON, DOUGLAS. "The Emerging Law of Student Rights." *Arkansas Law Review*. Vol. 23, 1970. Pp. 619-33. One of many articles appearing in various law reviews outlining the concepts which are changing so rapidly in the school situation and must influence the way administrators think and act.

CHAPTER 6

Legal Problems of Teachers

The most significant factor in the quality of any educational program is the adequacy of the teacher. In Colonial times this individual was likely to be both a teacher and a homemaker and was frequently referred to in the literature as someone who was willing to "keep" schools. At the secondary level the teacher was likely to be a clergyman or some other person who was educated for some other purpose or was using his teaching salary as a means to support himself while he "read" the law or prepared for some other professional calling. The development of teaching as a professional field began with the advent of teachers' colleges in the early 1840s in Massachusetts. These institutions were designed with training teachers as their primary function and popularized the notion that the schools would develop the most rapidly and with greater quality if persons would devote themselves to teaching as a "calling" with the same devotion and willingness to sacrifice as had clergy, or especially missionaries.

From time to time our society has become greatly concerned over the quality of the educational program. Various attempts to improve the system have included such things as professional certification, accreditation, retirement systems, graduate professional degrees, and sabbatical leaves for travel or study. As the educational program developed, litigation often has arisen to adjudicate the rights of the various parties involved in the enterprise. In terms of the number of transactions which occur everyday in the public schools of the United States, the incidence of lawsuits involving teachers is quite low. Although this be the case, the teacher who ventures into the "blackboard jungles" of today's urban areas must have a basic knowledge of the problems which arise in the schools and how to avoid the rudimentary situations out of which most court cases involving teachers develop. Preventive application of knowledge in these areas is highly desirable because the process of defending oneself in a case where one is named as defendant can be very expensive. A number of elements of educational practice where the courts have been involved in a sufficient number of cases to provide guidelines for professional practice will be examined and an analysis given to assist the prospective or practicing professional.

THE TEACHER'S CERTIFICATE

One of the first means that was used to develop professional standards and improve the teaching professional was the practice of certification. At first the standards which were utilized were based upon knowledges of subject matter and were given to all candidates who were able to pass an examination administered by some local officer, such as the county superintendent of schools. Modern programs of teacher certification are far more sophisticated and usually involve the student completing an approved program of teacher education in an accredited college and the state issuing an appropriate certificate for the grade level or subject for which the person prepared. Although widely criticized, certification has done more to improve the quality of education and to professionalize teaching than any other single device.

A considerable amount of litigation has arisen around the teacher's certificate. The process of certification is the legal device by which the state assures the public that the candidate who presents himself for a teaching position possesses the minimum personal and professional qualifications. The requirements established for acquiring a certificate may be changed by the state legislature from time to time to insure that the holder continues to be up to date in his knowledge and skills. The beginning teacher is often confused by the fact that each state has its own certificate law and when he moves from one state to another he finds that additional work may be necessary to meet the standards of that state. He may also find it difficult to move from one level to another because of similar difficulties. Although the certificate laws do screen out some worthy persons who would make acceptable teachers, they also protect the public against those individuals who would simply use teaching as a steppingstone to some other objective or persons who fail in some other field and want a teaching job as social security.

The teaching certificate is by its legal nature a "license," not a document conferring any kind of absolute right. The courts have consistently so classified the certificate so that the state might have the mandate to change its requirements without being confronted with the constitutional question of deprivation of property without due process of law. It does not guarantee employment, confer tenure, or even assure the individual who possesses one that it will be valid at some future date. Many states have statutory provisions which require the prospective teacher to have a certificate before entering into performance of a teaching contract or he may find that the school district is prohibited from drawing a payroll voucher until the teacher presents a valid certificate to the school officer who must file it for record purposes. Since possession of a certificate is one element of contractual capacity, a teacher who enters into teaching responsibility and who may be an excellent teacher cannot recover his or her salary unless a certificate is filed, and the courts usually declare a person who has not met the requirements to have been a "volunteer."

The state in granting a teaching certificate also imposes certain other limitations on it. It is a "personal privilege" granted by the state to an individual and because of this it cannot be transferred, sold, or bartered to any other individual. Its validity is usually limited to the subjects, grade levels, or position which is named on its face. Except in emergency situations, the practice of assigning teachers to positions for which they are not certified will bring about the cancellation of the school district's accreditation and in some cases may bring about the loss of state funds for the professional position in question. The person who accepts a certificate does so with the knowledge that he will be subject to subsequent changes brought about by the state legislature or the central education agency.

Certain benefits are assured to the person who is employed holding a valid certificate. When a teacher is employed it assures him that he will receive the salary which is stipulated in state minimum salary schedules or the salary schedules which are published by the local school board. The certificate is prima facie evidence of the holder's competency to do the work which is indicated by the training area which it represents. Should a board of education wish to dismiss a properly certificated individual on the grounds of incompetency, the burden of proof is upon the board to convince the court that such is the case. The certificate is not open to collateral attack. A teacher may not be dismissed on the grounds that the certificate that he holds was illegally issued. When properly issued and in his possession, the presumption is that certificate was legally issued and the person presenting it was qualified to hold it. Any attack on the certificate must be a direct one. The certificate also limits the right of the board of education to reassign or to transfer an employee. The courts usually approve reassignment for the benefit of the school district so long as the person is certified to fill that position to which he is assigned.

Teaching certificates are subject to cancellation by the central education agency or the state commissioner of education under the circumstances which are set out in the law of the state. In the Texas Education Code (Section 13.046) provision is made for cancellation under the following circumstances:

> (1) on satisfactory evidence that the holder is conducting his school or his teaching activities in violation of the laws of this state;
> (2) on satisfactory evidence that the holder is a person unworthy to instruct the youth of the state; or
> (3) on complaint made by the board of trustees that the holder of a certificate after entering into a valid contract with the board of trustees of the district has without good cause and without the consent of the trustees abandoned the contract.

Case law is available to enlarge upon each of these items. Suffice it to say that most legislatures and courts still consider teaching to be an exemplary profession and the teacher may be held to a higher standard of personal conduct than that expected of the average man on the street. Should any prospective teacher be tempted to attempt to alter his certificate in any way he should remember that many states include the altering of a teaching credential in the penal codes dealing with other forgeries, carrying a felony penalty in some states of as much as seven years.

THE TEACHER'S CONTRACT

The general characteristics of all contracts must be satisfied in those between a teacher and a school district. These five characteristics must be present: (1) the parties must have the capacity to contract, (2) the contract must be supported by a valid consideration, (3) the contract must be based upon mutual assent or the "meeting of the minds," (4) the rights and liabilities created by the contract must be definite enough to be enforceable, and (5) the contract must not contain subject matter that is illegal or against public policy. When a valid agreement has been reached between the teacher and the school trustees, certain rights and duties arise which may be enforced against each party. The mode of contracting for teaching positions is more extensively regulated by state statutes than are business contracts.

Basic to these regulations is the statutory prohibition of many states against oral contracts for teachers. This statutory provision usually speaks directly to the matter by saying, "all such contracts shall be in writing." The power to contract is resident in the board and may be exercised only at a regular or special meeting of the board when a quorum is present. Perhaps each of the basic elements of a contract should be discussed briefly.

Teachers, as well as other types of professionals who would contract in regard to providing professional services in their field, must be eligible to contract. In the educational profession this would mean that the teacher must be appropriately certified for the position for which he or she wishes to contract. The state also requires other factors as basic requirements for capacity to contract. These factors frequently include a minimum age, citizenship, no felony crime convictions, general health certificate, chest x-rays, maximum age, and in some, marital status. Since the only powers which a school board possesses are those which are conferred upon it by statute, persons who contract with the board are presumed to know the legal limitations under which the board operates and should be guided thereby. When the board attempts to contract in an "ultra vires" fashion, or attempts to go beyond its authority, the resulting agreement is void or of no legal effect.

Many problems arise because teachers often assume that they have a binding contract after they have agreed to an offer transmitted by the superintendent of schools. A superintendent, as an employee of the board, does not have the power to bind the district. The district is bound only after the board consummates such a contract and it is entered in the minutes of the board. Other incapacities may arise to contracting, as a teacher under nepotism statutes or conflict-of-interest statutes.

It is fundamental to the contracting process that the two parties understand and agree as to terms of the agreement. The nature of the transaction assumes that they bargain with each other until there is an exchange of promises of performance. One party usually makes an offer and the second party makes an acceptance. Since contracting is a recognized relationship of long standing in our society, certain rules have grown up around it. An offer may be extinguished by the occurrence of some event or the passing of time. After the offer expires, the acceptor can no longer accept it. At any time prior to an acceptance, the offer may be withdrawn by the offeror. An acceptance must be made in the mode and manner and within the time limitations which are contained in the offer.

It is also well to remember that a counter-offer extinguishes the prior offer. It often occurs that the acceptor attempts to bargain with the offeror by making a counter proposal to some aspect of the offer and then on refusal attempts to accept the original offer only to find that it has now been extinguished. It is also a well established rule that the intent of the parties will be determined by the overt acts of the parties not by some secret intent. The parol evidence rule will prohibit the use of oral testimony to determine the intent of the parties where the contract is an integrated document on its face. Many disagreements arise in school situations when a teacher maintains that the school administrator made an oral commitment which is contrary to the terms of the contract. The courts will not allow oral testimony to vary the terms of the written instrument. If your commitments are oral remember they are only moral commitments not legal ones.

Before any contract is enforceable there must be an exchange of valid considerations. This may be satisfied by an exchange of promises, an exchange of money for a promise, or the conferring of some benefit on the promisor while there is a loss or detriment to the promisee. When a valid consideration is lacking the contract is not consummated. An illustration which arose in a school situation is *State ex rel Melvin* v. *Board of Education of City of St. Bernard* (34 N.E. 2d 285, 1940). The local school board had passed a resolution attempting to extend the superintendent's contract some twenty-three months. The resolution failed to fix any compensation for the period. A new board came into office and was told by counsel that the prior board's resolution did not create a binding contract. In a hearing on a writ of mandamus to compel the board to continue to recognize him as superintendent the court found:

> No inference as to the amount of compensation can be drawn from the language used by the respondent in the resolution. . . . As an appointment without compensation . . . would not be binding upon the relator, neither would it be binding upon the respondent. There would be no consideration for the promise and, therefore, no binding contract.

Numerous other decisions would support this same opinion that where no valid consideration is exchanged there is no contract.

When a contract is drawn the terms of the contract must be sufficiently clear to be enforceable. When a teacher receives his contract he should examine it carefully with this problem in mind. Contracts with the following omissions have been invalidated by the courts: (1) a contract which purported to pay a teacher "good wages,"

(2) a contract which failed to give the beginning and ending dates for the period of service, (3) the grade of school or assignment being omitted and compensation to be paid, and (4) where the compensation to be paid was not determined before services were rendered. Should a question arise in this regard an attorney should be consulted.

In dealing with a school district a teacher seldom runs into a contract which has an unlawful subject matter. The most common type situation is probably one where a coach or athletic director is given an oral agreement for a multi-year period of service in a state which may or may not require a contract to be in writing. The statute of frauds in a state statute will normally require any contract which cannot be performed within one year to be in writing. A three-year oral contract would be against public policy and could not be enforced. Other states may prohibit the making of contracts on Sunday and most will not enforce contracts with aleatory or gambling provisions with the exception of insurance contracts. Each individual should have some knowledge of those contracts which are either illegal or against public policy in his state and avoid them.

EMPLOYEE RIGHTS OF TEACHERS

The employee relationship between a teacher and the school board is one that is little understood and does not have an equal in the business world. The familiar master-servant, principal-agent, or independent contractor arrangements by which most work relationships are described do not adequately describe a person who serves a school district in a professional capacity. Although his relationship is usually referred to as an employee as distinguished from an officer, public employees are frequently denied elements of behavior which their counterparts in the private sector might have as a matter of law or right. The right to organize and collectively bargain or to strike may be forbidden to public employees by state law.

Teachers are given preferential treatment under many state laws. If a teacher is properly certified and holds a valid contract with a district, payment of such teaching salary is primary to all other obligations of the district. If an individual teacher has not been paid under his contract, he may individually bring suit for payment and recover the amount which has not been paid. Teachers are also beneficiaries of the participation of the state in retirement systems. All states have some type of program to provide for teachers in their old age. The most common type is a joint-contributory annuity benefit. In this kind of program the individual and the state make equivalent contributions to a retirement fund from which benefits are paid whenever the teacher becomes disabled or reaches a specified age or period of service.

Although the local school board has the right to establish a salary schedule, it may not fall below the minimum schedule stipulated by the state legislature. This provision is ordinarily enforced by the central education agency of the state either by withdrawing accreditation or denying participation in state assistance for the support of local schools. Courts have generally denied classification for salary purposes based upon male-female, single-married, Negro-white, or dependents-no dependents. Classifications based upon subjective measures of performance have not been ruled out by the courts. In *Board of School Trustees* v. *Moore* (33 N.E. 2d 114, 1941) the Indiana Supreme Court permitted a salary schedule to stand which placed inefficient, uncooperative, and uninterested teachers in one category and placed the rest of the staff in another. Most of the actions taken by school boards must have some reasonable basis unless they are taken against the entire faculty in a similar fashion.

Teachers often complain about the extra work which often is required of them for which no extra remuneration is paid. Teachers' contracts often have what is called "elastic" clauses in them. The contract may read, "an addition to the general instructional duties, such other duties as the board or superintendent may direct." Such additional duties are included in the annual salary contract unless the contract stipulates that additional pay will be forthcoming for certain specialized activities. This concept was tested in *Parrish* v. *Moss* (106 N.Y.S. 2d 577, 1951), where a group of teachers attempted to force a school board to pay additional salary for extra duties that had been assigned. The court upheld the board saying:

> The hours of service of its teachers may not necessarily coincide with the hours of classroom instruction, nor is it legally required that the hours fixed be the same for all teachers. . . . A board is not required to pay additional compensation for such services. The duty assigned must be within the scope of teacher's duties. Teachers may not be required, for instance, to perform janitor service, police service. . . . These are not teaching duties.

The press of clerical and other non-teaching duties has led many teacher organizations to make an issue for collective negotiation out of such requirements. The Master Agreement between the Cherry Hill

Education Association and the Cherry Hill Board of Education, 1970-72, in Michigan has the following statement:

> D. No teacher shall be required to work beyond the time stated above. It is understood that in a few cases the Association recognizes that there should be a measure of voluntary participation without compensation on the part of the professional staff. These should be held to minimum, and where possible, these functions shall be performed during the school day.

Several of such agreements have specific duties which do not draw additional pay, and stipulate that all others shall be paid. In the past it has been assumed that teachers should give many evenings at home to lesson planning, grading of papers, and other chores associated with the profession. The new breed of teacher is likely to continue to protest expecting the teacher to spend as much of his own time with school chores. Other common complaints include having a supervisory assignment during the entire school day without a break from the time the children arrive in the morning until they leave in the evening, having no lunchbreak, supervising the loading of buses, hall monitoring, and playground supervision. The trend toward using nonprofessional teacher aides in many of these assignments should provide the teacher time for planning, design of teaching materials, evaluation, and clerical activities on school time during the regular day.

The rules and regulations of a board of trustees, the state education code, and rules of a central education agency become a part of the teacher's contract by a legal doctrine of adhesion. If a board requires every teacher to undertake a refresher course in a college or university, it may enforce such policy through its salary schedule by awarding or denying increments for that purpose. If the board has an official leave policy for maternity, illness, professional growth, sabbaticals, or death in the family, these benefits become contractual benefits. Courts will also enforce reasonable rules or regulations even if they are passed after the contract for a given year has been signed. Such rules may apply to holding other employment while teaching, especially if the second job had some type of moral connotation to it or interfered with the teacher's regular classroom duties.

TENURE RIGHTS OF TEACHERS

Two different types of legislation have passed state legislatures during recent years that have sought to give the teacher additional protection beyond that of term contracts. Although the term contract gave a maximum amount of freedom to both parties to renegotiate employment at the end of its term, teachers and other school employees felt that the school board held too much power in that it could simply refuse to renew a teacher's contract at the end of his or her period of service. The professional groups as a result have attempted to get legislation passed to provide some equalization of power in the contracting process. The result has been to pass either a teacher tenure statute or a continuing contract statute. The effect of both kinds of legislation is to provide greater protection for the teacher in connection with changes in board membership or philosophy. These statutes generally call for a probationary period of service where the incoming teacher is required to demonstrate teaching effectiveness. The period of probation usually provides three years of observation and evaluation of the teacher's performance. After this period is successfully served the teacher achieves tenure status.

The tenure teacher's contract is normally renewed automatically if the employing board does not notify the teacher in writing by the first day of April. Should the board notify the teacher of impending separation, the teacher has the right to request a public hearing on the matter. The reasons for dismissal are listed in the statute and are serious matters such as: conviction on a felony charge, incompetency, drunkenness, immorality, abuse of corporal punishment, or similar charges. If the teacher is unhappy with the dismissal procedures he may request further administrative proceedings with the state commissioner of education or state board of education and have judicial review if desirable.

Although this type of legislation is of recent origin, it has done much to stablilize the teaching profession. It has fostered the rise of professionalism and has permitted teaching to attract and retain teachers who serve long enough in a given community to know its children and serve them better. There are many who criticize the tenure statutes, saying that the procedures for separation are so cumbersome that they protect the marginal or weak teacher. From the teacher's point of view, the previous relationship of serving at the board's pleasure placed their jobs in annual jeopardy and frequent complaints of arbitrary or capricious discharge were heard.

Tenure laws always produce a sequence of litigation. The only way that the language and limits of such legislation may be tested is through court action. School administrators and school boards nearly always resist the granting of new authority to teachers. They would prefer to continue to employ or discharge teachers at will. In the first few years after new legislation passes many disputes as to meaning arise and resolution is only possible through the formal means of resolving social conflict. In addition to formal resolution, more teachers' organizations are resorting to other methods of settlement such as strikes, sick-outs, sanctions, or other forms of social action.

PERSONAL OR POLITICAL RIGHTS OF TEACHERS

The history of public education is replete with illustrations that teachers have not enjoyed the same personal, political, or professional rights as those exercised by persons engaged in other professions. Many efforts have been put forth in the past to remedy this situation. The effort of various professional groups representing educators and litigation by individual educators has made significant progress in the last decade in asserting and establishing teacher rights. Teachers have often been included in the same category as governmental workers, members of the armed services, and postal workers and have had limitations placed upon them because of their unique status. The exemplary nature of the profession has caused boards of trustees and even the courts to feel that they are justified in holding teachers to higher standards of behavior than the ordinary citizen. These traditional positions have caused many persons in public education to feel that they are "second-class" citizens. Many school boards have also contributed to this feeling by the arbitrary actions that they could and did take with little concern because the average teacher would accept various outrageous discriminations without reaction. Teachers often reacted with a sense of futility because to appeal meant personal expense for attorneys and the familiar 'blackball" in connection with other employment if they were labeled "troublemakers."

The picture described in the previous paragraph has changed significantly and will continue to change. These changes have been brought about by three significant factors: (1) legislative changes, (2) significant court decisions, and (3) more militant professional organizations. A brief discussion of each of these factors will give considerable insight into this problem.

The legislative effort involved the profession attempting to move on several fronts but the success achieved varied considerably from state to state. In a number of states sponsored bills made it unlawful for an administrator or board to attempt to exert influence on the teacher's choice of whether or not to join a particular professional organization or to participate in the political affairs of his community. The Texas Education Code (Section 21.904, Requiring or Coercing Teachers to Join Groups, Clubs, Committees, or Organizations: Political Affairs) has an excellent illustration of this type of legislation and it states:

> (a) No school district, board of education, superintendent, assistant superintendent, principal, or other administrator benefiting by the funds provided for in this code shall directly or indirectly require or coerce any teacher to join any group, club, committee, organization, or association.
> (b) It shall be the responsibility of the State Board of Education to notify every superintendent of schools in every district of the state of the provisions of this section.
> (c) It shall be the responsibility of the State Board of Education to enforce the provisions of this section.
> (d) No school district, board of education, superintendent, assistant superintendent, principal, or other administrator shall directly or indirectly coerce any teacher to refrain from participating in political affairs in his community, state or nation.

Such coercion had been carried on in a variety of ways. One common manner was to pressure teachers to join a particular professional organization because the district had a record of 100 percent membership and the district wished to maintain it. Other districts would solicit campaign contributions for trustee elections or bond elections from school employees. Other teachers reported that they had been warned not to support various political candidates or participate actively in political campaigning. Individual teachers and teacher organizations have had the courage to assert their personal and political rights under such statutes.

Successful court cases have also contributed to the increased personal rights of the members of the teaching profession. The landmark decision in this area was the case of *Tinker* v. *Des Moines Independent Community School District* (393 U.S. 503, 1969), in which the disciplinary rules of the district in regard to the wearing of black arm bands was tested. Justice Fortas in delivering the majority opinion states, "It can hardly be argued that either students or teachers shed their constitutional rights at the schoolhouse gate." The opinion makes it clear that First Amendment rights should be available to both students and faculty even though the schools were a special kind of environment. This decision added impetus to the many suits that had already been filed under the *Brown* v. *Board of Education* (349 U.S. 294, 1955) case in regard to the desegregation of schools. In a landmark Fifth Circuit Court of Appeals case styled *United States* v. *Jefferson County Board of Education* (380 F. 2d 385, 1966) the court stated:

> (a) Faculty Employment. Race or color shall not be a factor in the hiring, assignment, reassignment, promotion, demotion, or dismissal of teachers and other professional staff members, including student teachers, except that race may be taken into account for the purpose of counteracting or correcting the effect of segregated assignment of faculty and staff in the dual system. . . .
>
> (b) Dismissals. Teachers and other professional staff members may not be discriminatorily assigned, dismissed, demoted, or passed over for retention, promotion, or rehiring on the ground of race or color. . . .

This decision, among others, established the "equal protection" doctrine for all personnel actions taken in a local school distrct. It is now well established that the Fourteenth Amendment applies to all actions taken by a local school board as an agent of the state.

In most states teachers as public employees do not have the same rights as employees in the private sector. Particularly is this true in regard to collective actions such as strikes. The tool used by most school boards in attacking such action is an injunction. In at least two cases the teachers' organizations attempted to bring the various activities of strike action, such as inducing others to join the effort, under the First Amendment speech activities and protections. The courts of Michigan and Ohio rejected such arguments, indicating that under the police power of the state reasonable restrictions were not forbidden and free speech must be predicated on the lawful exercise of such right. In fact under several laws, if the public employee group claims to have the right to strike it loses its right to representation before the public board which employs it. Both teacher professional groups and union teacher groups have indicated that they will seek legislative action in a number of states seeking to strengthen the role of teachers both professionally and personally.

Since *Tinker* teachers have made great strides in having other rights recognized by the courts and then accepted by many school boards and administrators. The use of tests such as the National Teachers Examination and the Graduate Record Examination to determine selection or retention of teachers has been declared a violation of due process, since they do not purport to measure factors related to success as a teacher. A New York case, *Chance* v. *Board of Examiners* (330 F. Supp. 203, 1971), declared that competitive tests for administrative and supervisory positions were lawful only if they measure fairly the knowledge or skills necessary for the job or class of jobs for which the applicant is a candidate. However, if the candidate has a reputation as a militant both on and off the campus of the college he attended, an administrator may refuse to permit him to participate in student teaching, thereby effectively screening such individual out of the profession. The court in *James* v. *West Virginia Board of Regents* (22 F. Supp. 217, 1971) said:

> On the evidence this court has no difficulty in finding that it affords a reasonable hypothesis for the school officials to conclude, as they did, that plaintiff would not be a fit and proper person, characterwise, to be entrusted with the important task of teaching the young in this county.

Other courts have also said the local board could establish standards of physical fitness as well. A Texas court in *Montgomery* v. *White* (320 F. Supp. 303, 1969) upset the notion that classroom conduct alone must be the sole criterion of the effectiveness or fitness of a teacher. The state was declared to have the right to investigate the competency and fitness of those whom it hires to teach in its schools.

Teachers have discovered that school boards could not enforce a policy which prohibited their participation or involvement in any political activity other than voting. Continued employment could not be based upon or conditioned upon surrender of rights or refused because of the exercise of one's rights. Boards have also determined that the courts will require them to use or impose the same minimum requirements or utilize the same objective non-discriminatory standards in appointment, assignment, and dismissal of teachers. School districts have also had decisions to dismiss personnel reversed where they were based on discrimination, capriciousness, unreasonable grounds, or mere personal preference.

Although school boards have a widely recognized discretionary authority, its use has been curtailed by the courts where it has been used in an unconstitutional manner. Denial of tenure status because a teacher exercised First Amendment rights in expressing an opinion that "the school administrators were trying to buy the teachers off with little items at the expense of big ones" at a negotiating session has been reversed. Teachers have also found considerable relief from rules governing grooming and personal appearance. In *Ramsey* v. *Hawkins* (320 F. Supp. 477, 1970) the burden of proof of showing a mustache was disruptive of the educational process, or was unhealthful, was placed upon the school board where it sought to terminate the teacher's employment for violation of its no-mustache rule.

Teachers who have tenure can expect a notice of dismissal and may have a hearing before the board. Even untenured teachers may have hearings where they can show that they have been dismissed for constitutionally impermissible reasons. Teachers have been moderately successful in establishing academic freedom. One court indicated that the right to teach, to inquire, to evaluate, and to study is fundamental to a democratic society. It added that academic freedom is not an absolute, and that an assignment must bear some relationship to a recognized educational goal.

SUMMARY

The teaching profession has made tremendous strides in its attempts to create a professional group whose primary aim is to contribute teachers' professional careers to the improvement of public education. During the early period of education in New England most of the teaching was done by "dames" or housewives, clergymen, or other persons who possessed some educational training. In many frontier communities an itinerant teacher might serve a number of families by traveling among them. The profession took on much of its present character when many of the states passed laws requiring that the person who desires to teach must possess a certificate. The intent behind the certificate was to protect the public against those who were not minimally prepared to serve in the schools. Such certificates are merely licenses which can be canceled for cause, can be updated as to requirements, and can be changed by legislative action.

Teacher tenure and continuing contract laws have contributed greatly to the stability of the teachers' position. These laws have protected the teachers from arbitrary or capricious removal from their positions after they served a probationary period in the employing school. In addition to these statutory protections, teachers have also benefited from more aggressive professional organizations that take an active interest in the teachers' welfare and conditions of employment. Through the professional negotiation statutes, teacher organizations have established a formal means of communication with the school board and have an opportunity to air their grievances and find solutions to them in a professional manner. The courts have also taken an active role in defining and protecting the teachers' professional and constitutional rights. Court proceedings have become another avenue of utilized means to protect the role of the professional educator.

SELECTED BIBLIOGRAPHY

Books

HAZARD, WILLIAM R. *Education and the Law.* New York: The Free Press, 1971. 480 pages. The author in this text uses an unusual approach of text, readings, and case materials for his discussion of "Teacher-Board Relations" in Chapter 5.

National Education Association. *The Teacher's Day in Court: A Review of 1971.* Washington, D.C.: National Education Association—Research Division, 1972. 131 pages. The N.E.A. publishes this Research Report annually and it touches the most significant cases involving teachers or other certificated personnel. The report is arranged by state with a short digest of the important cases.

NOLTE, M. CHESTER. *Guide to School Law.* West Nyack, N.Y.: Parker Publishing Co., 1969. 238 pages. This text has some excellent discussion of the political and personal rights of employees in education. It would provide an excellent source for persons without an extensive background in school law.

NOLTE, M. CHESTER, and JOHN PHILLIP LINN. *School Law for Teachers.* Danville, Ill.: Interstate Printers & Publishers, 1964. 343 pages. Although this book was written sometime ago, Chapter 7, "Political and Personal Rights of Teachers," is a well written text and worth reading, although it does not reflect the most recent cases.

PETERSON, LEROY J., ed. *Yearbook of School Law 1972.* Topeka, Kan.: National Organization on Legal Problems of Education, 1972. 260 pages. The Yearbook reviews several hundred cases dealing with problems which have arisen in public schools and been appealed to appellate courts or have been heard in trial courts of record. "Teachers and Other Employees" is a section which is well worth reading.

Periodicals

BEHLING, HERMAN E., JR. "The Legal Gravity of Specific Acts in Cases of Teacher Dismissal." *North Dakota Law Review.* Vol. 43, No. 4 (Summer 1967). Pp. 753-63. This article gives an interesting analysis of the kinds of acts which result in a teacher's dismissal on single or repeated acts. It provides some insights into the kinds of behavior which school boards will not tolerate from teachers.

DELON, FLOYD G. *Substantive Legal Aspects of Teacher Discipline.* Topeka, Kan.: National Organization on Legal Problems in Education, 1972. 73 pages. An interesting and informative monograph on the substantive due process issues in connection with teacher discipline and dismissal. The author analyzes a change of attitude toward being more liberal in regulations governing teacher behavior.

HUBERT, FRANK W. R. "Dismissal of Public School Employees in Texas—Suggestions for a More Effective Process." *Texas Law Review.* 44:1309, 1966. A comment which concludes with recommended policies to control administrative practices in regard to dismissal of public employees. The basic law discussed in the article is Texas law but the conclusions have wide applicability.

PUNKE, HAROLD H. "Insubordination in Teacher Dismissal." *Michigan Bar Journal.* August 1966. Pp. 51-60. An easily read article which concentrates on various acts which fall in the insubordination area or one which is closely related, such as neglect of duty or unfitness to teach. The discussion of the legal definition of insubordination is particularly important to teachers or teacher organizations.

"What Constitutes 'Incompetency' or 'Inefficiency' as a Ground for Dismissal or Demotion of Public School Teacher." 4 *American Law Reports 3d* 1090. This article is the most extensive annotation available on the subject. An undergraduate student or someone unfamiliar with this reference work may need assistance to use it. It covers topics as varied as obesity to criticism of a superior as grounds for dismissal.

CHAPTER 7

Students' Rights on Campus

The American college and secondary school campuses have been swept by a tide of student unrest which has brought about widespread public concern as to the nature of the relationships that have been maintained between the academic community and its student clientele. Legislative bodies have reacted to this violence by enacting tough new statutes on campus disruption and loitering. The disruption laws were designed to arm judicial and administrative authorities with a means of dealing with militant student groups who took physical control of campus buildings, imprisoned faculty members or administrators in their offices, disrupted student assemblies by chanting four-letter obscenities, burning or otherwise damaging buildings, and fostering student boycott of classes. Conviction on a charge of disruption could lead to significant fines and/or jail terms and repeated conviction could bar attendance at a tax-supported institution for periods of two years. The loitering statutes were designed to keep non-students off campus so that the resources of student groups, both money and manpower, could not be so easily manipulated by professional organizers. These statutes typically give an administrative officer the authority to challenge the right to be on campus. If the person challenged did not have a legitimate right to be on campus the administrator could request him to leave and if he did not he could have him arrested on a charge of loitering. Some state legislatures also reacted to the violence and unrest by ordering campus investigations and cutting state funds.

Sociologists, social psychologists, congressional committees, presidential commissions, and other groups have attempted to study and evaluate the social and educational climate which would foster such confrontation between the "establishment" and student groups. Participation by students in school or university governance, the communication "gap," suppression of the new life-style of the devotees of the counter-culture, the frustration of a long-term military conflict which had become unpopular with a sizable segment of the population, and other problems surfaced in these studies or analyses of the educational scene. Whether the conflict was at the secondary or collegiate level, student leaders and militant student groups quickly learned that the educational institutions were not prepared to respond either psychologically or physically to confrontation and violence. A handful of college security personnel whose primary preoccupation had been enforcement of parking regulations could not cope with hundreds of students who became noisy, jeering, and destructive mobs. The local police, sheriff's deputies, state police, or military groups were similarly ill-prepared to deal with this kind of problem. Campus issues frequently merged with civil rights, women's liberation, anti-war, political, or other groups who were intent upon some type of mission in regard to modifying or destroying the "system." In the heat of such activity it is often difficult to assess the impact of a given force or the validity of a response born of gut reaction or experience. It appears that during periods of lull or reduced activity which generally follow sustained high-level periods that some calm reflection should be turned toward such social processes for the purpose of ordering chaos and harnessing energies toward constructive and controlled change.

AN ORDERED EDUCATIONAL ENVIRONMENT

Most educators would probably agree that the educational process must contain some constructs which produce an environment conducive to the achievement of educational goals. The conditions for learning activities, whether they are free school or traditional school in orientation, require some philosophical or conceptual framework upon which educational objectives are structured to accomplish certain goals. The educational scene in America has been influenced heavily for more than two centuries by the doctrine of "in loco parentis." This theory of school or college administration tends to produce a system which is paternalistic in nature and fosters the arbitrary exercise of authority on the part of those who are occupying positions of power. Such unilateral exercise of authority has been the basis of protest by many students and faculty members during this period of student activism. Persons who are planning for careers as professional educators or who already occupy positions of professional responsibility in education must thoughtfully consider this problem area.

The normal course of analysis would require the inquirer to ask the question, "How much system or order is required for the school or college to function?" The constitutional mandate which is delegated to educational authorities generally stipulates that an efficient system of free public schools should be maintained. Judicial guidelines for decision making have generally followed the broad discretionary grants of authority by legislative groups in regard to making rules and regulations for school functioning. The courts went so far as to erect legal presumptions that school regulations dutifully and lawfully made were "reasonable" rules and required the person who complained to rebut such presumption. The broad grants of discretionary authority and their bulwarking by judicial construction have become the "seed bed" for a great deal of controversy and litigation. The question of "what behaviors ought the school control?" of necessity must arise. The nature of the educational programs dictates certain kinds of behavioral control systems. Some limits would appear to be:

1. Behaviors which actually disrupt the ongoing educational process.
2. Behaviors which are aggressive and have the potential to physically injure others.
3. Behaviors which lead to destruction of school facilities or property.
4. Behaviors which interfere with the administrative functions of the school, that is, student traffic, housekeeping, health, or safety.
5. Behaviors which are unlawful or contribute to the breakdown of law enforcement.

Most of the resources which have been used by the courts for guidance were derived from educational sources. As a result, the judicial precedents available from legal literature or case law were strongly dependent upon a broadly and loosely interpreted notion of parental-like control possessed by school authority. These decisions conferred almost unlimited control of in-school behaviors and extended it out-of-school to behaviors which reflected upon the educational program. In a 1968 case, *Epperson* v. *Arkansas* (393 U.S. 97, 1968), the United States Supreme Court again indicated its reluctance to serve as a super-school board when it declared that it would not intervene in resolution of conflicts or daily problems. The federal courts have not been reluctant, however, to intervene where the authority of school administrators or districts has been used in an unreasonable, arbitrary, or capricious manner.

THE BILL OF RIGHTS ON THE CAMPUS

Looking back at constitutional law decisions of the past two centuries, one is made to wonder why the rights of minors or children under the Bill of Rights of the United States Constitution had not been clearly delineated. The leap forward for students in the rights area occurred in 1965 in a case styled *In re Gault* (387 U.S. 1, 1965). Although this case was not in an educational setting, it has had a profound effect upon educational theory and practice. The case actually involved a juvenile offender who had been arrested for making obscene telephone calls. After his hearing he was sentenced to a state correctional institution for a period of six years. An adult committing the same offense would have gotten a few months in jail and a small fine. The severity of the penalty had been influenced greatly by the appellant's personal statements. In noting a concern for the procedural irregularities Justice Fortas, reversing the conviction, noted simply that children too should have the protection of constitutional safeguards. The impact of this Court's opinion has not been fully explored by the judiciary as to how these newly announced rights will function in many areas.

The issue which brought the relationship between the school and its student clientele into focus was that of an anti-Vietnam war demonstration. Several children whose families were concerned about the nation's involvement in the war decided to have their children wear black arm bands to school in a protest which was calling for moratorium in the conflict. When the students appeared at school wearing the arm bands, they were suspended on the basis of a school regulation which was of recent origin. The parents sued the school district, claiming the constitutional rights of their children had been abridged. In *Tinker* v. *Des Moines Independent Community School District* (393 U.S. 503, 1969), with Justice Fortas again writing the majority opinion, the United States Supreme Court announced that even in the light of the special needs of the school environment neither teachers nor children left the constitutional rights at the "schoolhouse gate." The black arm bands were declared to be "symbolic speech" and were declared to be under First Amendment protections. The Court placed considerable weight on the fact that the activity which the school sought to regulate had not caused any significant disruption nor had the school any history of conflict or disruptive activity. The Court more importantly established a "balancing test" which was to guide school authorities when seeking to regulate student behavior in constitutionally protected interests. The interests which are in conflict are the right of the students to be protected in constitutionally assured areas of behavior and the necessity of the state to maintain an efficient system of public schools. When the student meets the burden of showing the state it is intruding into an area of constitutionally protected activity, the burden of proof shifts to the state to show some compelling reason for establishing rules and regulations in this area. The courts have insisted that these rules be based upon something more than vague fears or unpopular positions or attitudes being expressed. The most frequently cited justification for attempted regulation in the rights area has been that of "disruption." Testimony that such rules were preventive in nature has not been received by most courts unless a "clear and present danger" has been shown. Much confusion exists in this area of student rights because of the dissimilar rulings of the federal Circuit Courts of Appeals. In spite of the problem of reconciling the varying opinions it seems that the Bill of Rights is firmly established on the campus and that subsequent decisions may explore the boundaries of its application in the educational situation.

THE DISRUPTIVE STUDENT

Until recently the courts have given an almost unlimited support for authoritarian or autocratic use of authority in an educational situation. In court decisions of the early nineteenth century it was not uncommon for courts to refuse jurisdiction in educational controversies at all, indicating that relief of the nature sought must be found in the power of the polls or in the halls of the legislature. The loose way in which the courts interpreted "in loco parentis" added legal presumptions of reasonableness to all rules and regulations instituted by lawfully constituted boards of education. Statutes were passed which embodied this philosophy and they were bulwarked by the judicial precedents which were stacked on top of them. Some early decisions sought to reverse this trend. In the 1943 *West Virginia State Board of Education* v. *Barnette* case (319 U.S. 624, 1943), the oppressive use of state authority in enacting a state statute which required under penalty of expulsion for each child to participate in a morning exercise which required a flag salute was declared unconstitutional. In striking down the state statute the Court declared:

> The Fourteenth Amendment, as now applied to the states, protects the citizen against all the creatures of the state.... Boards of Education included.... These have, of course, important delicate, and highly discretionary functions but none which they may not perform within the limits of the Bill of Rights.

Although there were other scattered cases where the courts refused to follow the guidance of educational authorities, the majority of cases continued to rely upon the expertise of those who administered schools to guide their decisions. The most significant change in the courts' attitudes began with the *Brown* v. *Board of Education* case (347 U.S. 483, 1954), which overturned the "separate but equal" doctrine in connection with racially segregated facilities which were required by state law. When force and violence were used to attempt to maintain racially segregated schools the Court again spoke in *Cooper* v. *Aaron* (358 U.S. 1, 1958), declaring that "law and order are not here to be preserved by depriving children of their constitutional rights." A general decline in judicial support has occurred for the arbitrary use of authority to suppress the constitutional rights of children who were enrolled in the public schools. By the late 1960s the deference once shown to the opinions and desires of school authorities declined to the point that the Court recognized that it had a duty to intervene where the Fourteenth Amendment and other rights were being infringed. Some authorities in public schools began to attack the lack of democracy in the schools.

For both the school administrator and the courts it has been difficult to delineate the boundaries of the right of the student to exhibit certain kinds of behavior and when such behavior interferes with the rights of others to the degree that it becomes disruptive and should be regulated or suppressed. This represents another of the areas of debate in our society where competing interests are in conflict. Where the student has engaged in aggressive behavior, destroyed property, has been insubordinate, or has actually disrupted the educational program the courts have seldom intervened. In spite of the legal responsibility which rests upon those who are in positions of governance, educational criteria which look at disruption or other processes involved in changing educational programs as educational rather than destructive forces must be developed. It appears that many of the courts have seized upon the differences in cultures and life-styles as possessing educational potential more rapidly than have educators. Perhaps an examination of the treatment provided by the courts in student litigation will give us a better insight than other approaches.

STUDENTS AND THE FIRST AMENDMENT

The cases which have arisen in an educational setting interpreting the rights guaranteed against the Congress have fallen into at least five areas. These areas are (1) the establishment of religion clause, (2) the free exercise clause, (3) the freedom of speech clause, (4) the freedom of the press clause, and (5) the clause guaranteeing the right to peaceably assemble and petition the government for a redress of grievances. Since the prohibitions which are expressed in this amendment are directed toward Congress, as a practical matter a litigant in this area will of necessity, when suing a college or public school district, tie this amendment to the Fourteenth, which forbids any state to make or enforce any law which shall abridge the privileges or immunities of a citizen of the United States. The decisions which have been made pursuant to this area have brought about widespread changes in administrative practice in the schools.

RELIGION AND THE SCHOOLS

The current era in interpretation of the "establishment of religion" clause has brought about the recognition of at least four expressions of legal philosophy. The Founding Fathers felt that freedom of religion was perhaps the single great motivating factor in guiding the colonists to seek a new home. Religious intolerance in the Colonies soon brought about a recognition that a complete separation of church and state was essential. Early theorists insisted that there should be a "wall of separation," high and impregnable, between church and state. Even though this concept was given widespread acceptance the religious practices which had crept into the public schools had seldom been challenged, perhaps because of somewhat homogeneous religious outlooks in various communities whose constituents felt that various kinds of religious practices should be a part of the daily school program. In early litigation the courts generally held that Bible reading and general prayer were not sectarian in nature and did not violate religious guarantees.

The "pupil benefit" theory represents one variation of the original concepts in this area. Even though the majority of states do not accept this concept, in at least two areas several states have accepted expenditure of public funds to assist students who were enrolled in parochial schools. In *Cochran* v. *Louisiana State Board of Education* (281 U.S. 370, 1930) the Court determined that a state plan to provide textbooks for parochial school students did not violate the Fourteenth Amendment. The Court accepted the argument that the state's appropriation was made for the specific purpose of purchasing school books for the use of the school children of the state free of cost to them. The schools were not the beneficiaries of the appropriation and obtained nothing from it nor were they relieved of any obligation because of it. The decision included the following language: "We cannot doubt that in this case the taxing power of the state is exerted for a public purpose." This doctrine has also been accepted in several states in decisions relating to school transportation. The leading case, *Everson* v. *Board of Education* (330 U.S. 1, 1947), involved the issue of reimbursement of parents for transportation expenses whose children attended parochial schools. The Court stated that use of public funds to provide funds for transportation of all children to school worked for a public purpose. The majority felt that the state statute had not breached the wall of separation which must be kept "high and impregnable."

The second line of cases developed about the concern that the "released time" or "dismissed time" concepts violated the "neutrality" to religion position adopted by the Court. Two cases have stood for two decades as the landmarks in this area. In *McCollum* v. *Board of Education* (33 U.S. 203, 1948), a released time education program was declared unconstitutional. In this case the pupils were released from classes to attend religious instruction conducted by locally provided teachers in school classrooms while others stayed in study halls or continued to pursue secular studies. A "dismissed time" situation was upheld in *Zorach* v. *Clauson* (343 U.S. 306, 1952), where New York City permitted students to be dismissed during the school day so that they might leave the campus and go to religious centers for religious instruction and devotional exercises. The student was released upon the request of his parents. Those who were not released continued their regular schedule of activities. Since the program was voluntary and all expense was carried without the expenditure of public funds, the Supreme Court felt it had no reason to intervene and should not show hostility to religion.

Another area of concern to school administrators has been that of prayer and Bible reading in public school classrooms. Much legislative and judicial controversy has been engendered in this area. A significant series of cases began in this area with the *Engel* v. *Vitale*

(370 U.S. 421, 1962), concerning the "Regents' Prayer." An interfaith prayer, "Almighty God, we acknowledge our dependence upon Thee, and we by Thy blessing upon us, our parents, our teachers, and our country," had been designated by the New York state Board of Regents to be used as a part of a devotional activity at the beginning of each day. The Court felt that "religion is too personal, too sacred, too holy, to permit its unhallowed perversion by a civil magistrate," and invalidated the practice as a violation of the Establishment Clause. Shortly after the prayer case the Supreme Court was called upon again to interpret the Establishment Clause. The states of Pennsylvania and Maryland had statutes which required the reading of ten verses from the Holy Bible without comment at the beginning of the school day and reading of one chapter without comment and-or the use of the Lord's Prayer, respectively. Each had a provision that children who did not wish to participate could be excused. The Court concluded that in both cases the laws required religious exercises and that such exercises were being conducted in violation of law. In face of a criticism that the Court was establishing a religion of secularism, it said "we agree that the state may not establish a religion of secularism in the sense of affirmatively opposing or showing hostility to religion, thus favoring or preferring those who believe in no religion over those who do believe." The "strict neutrality" doctrine in which the government can neither favor nor oppose religious practice became established. Although some cases in state courts have not followed the strict interpretation by the United States Supreme Court of the Establishment Clause, the federal courts have followed it consistently.

In *West Virginia Board of Education* v. *Barnette* (319 U.S. 624, 1943), the matter of "conscience" seems also to be protected by the Fourteenth Amendment application of the First Amendment. In this case a state statute requiring, upon threat of expulsion, an affirmation of the pledge of allegiance as a daily exercise was overturned. The Court held that where patriotism and religious scruples conflict that the right of religious freedom should prevail. Similarly in *Wisconsin* v. *Yoder* (92 S. Ct. 1526, 1971), the Court ruled that the compulsory attendance law of the state of Wisconsin must yield to a religious practice which maintains an eighth-grade educational program of an old order Amish religious community. The "neutrality" concept was used as the basis for a petition where a citizen sought to force a public community college student newspaper publishing articles from attacking religious groups or figures. The court said, "a student newspaper, tax-supported, must not be inimical to the institutions its parent government is required to leave alone." This case, *Panarella* v. *Birenbaum* (302 N.Y.S. 2d 427, 1969) although later reversed, resulted in orders given to the president and governing boards of the colleges involved that "would prevent publication of such articles by enforcement of existing regulations, enactment of new ones or otherwise." As a curriculum matter, these decisions do not prohibit the use of a Bible course in public school curriculum. In a decision (*Epperson* v. *State of Arkansas*, 393 U.S. 97, 1968) the United States Supreme Court indicated that so long as the Bible course was taught from a historical, literary, or factual point of view the Court would not intervene. A wide range of matters has been listed under these clauses of the federal Constitution and as a general matter activities which bring about "excessive entanglement" between the affairs of church and state have been forbidden.

FREEDOM OF SPEECH IN A CAMPUS ENVIRONMENT

Freedom of speech protected by the First Amendment and Fourteenth Amendment is not absolute and has generally been held to be subject to constitutional restrictions for the protection of the social interests in government, order, and morality. The courts have been reluctant to stifle speech but have announced in several cases a test of how far the right extends. In *Schwartz* v. *Schuker* (298 F. Supp. 238, 1964) the transcript contains the following dicta:

> While there is a certain aura of sacredness attached to the First Amendment, nevertheless the First Amendment rights must be balanced against the duty and obligations of the state to educate students in an orderly and decent manner to protect the rights not of the few but all of the students in the school system. The line of reason must be drawn somewhere in this area of ever expanding permissibility.

It has required considerable litigation to determine where this line of reason exists and how to convert the abstract right into one of student expression. Student expression in general will be upheld unless the language used is excessively abusive, disruptive, or is designed to create gross disrespect or contempt for the educational situation.

The Court has been willing to protect "expression of opinion which is conveyed without materially and substantially interfering with the appropriate discipline of the school" (*Tinker* v. *Des Moines School District*, 393 U.S. 503, 1969). Standards often quoted from cases outside a school environment include the "clear and present" criterion and "whether the gravity of the evil, discounted by its improbability, justified such invasion of free speech as is necessary to avoid the danger." Use of restrictive rules by school administrators to stifle expression of opinion has been discouraged. In *Tinker* the Court emphasized that prohibiting speech or expression on the basis of an undifferentiated fear or apprehension of disturbance would not be supported. Activities which are closely akin to speech, such as black arm bands or wearing buttons or insignia as pictorial speech, are often tolerated by the courts unless there has been an atmosphere of violence or disruption. As the non-verbal message becomes more remote, the justification for substantial protection of the First Amendment declines.

Students often wonder how far they may go in the area of expression. A minimum standard of propriety and accepted norms of social or public behavior may be enforced (*Goldberg* v. *Regents of University of California*, 248 Cal. Rptr. 2d 867, 1967). In addition to the time-worn standard of shouting "fire" in a crowded theater, courts have added other restrictions such as: "fighting words which inflict injury by utterance" (*Chaplinsky* v. *New Hampshire* 315 U.S. 568, 1942); "gross disrespect and contempt for officials of an educational institution" (*Schwartz* v. *Schuker*, 298 F. Supp. 238, 1969); where the school authorities are in "circumstances which offer them no practical alternatives" to extinguishment of constitutional rights (*Butts* v. *Dallas Independent School District* 436 F. 2d 728, rev. 306 F. Supp. 488, 1969); where buttons were distributed forcibly through school windows (*Burnside* v. *Byers*, 363 F. 2d 744, 1966); "abrasive and contemptuous behavior" (*Lipkis* v. *Caveney*, 96 Cal. Rptr. 779, 1971); "singing or marching in the hall during school hours" (*Hill* v. *Lewis*, 323 F. Supp. 55, 1971); or "using profanity in school" (*Ferrell* v. *Dallas Independent School District*, 261 F. Supp. 545, 1966). Whatever control school or college authorities attempt to exercise in this area should have a legitimate governmental purpose and they may find themselves required to come forward with a substantial showing of a necessary relationship of their regulation to a compelling state interest.

WHAT ABOUT THE STUDENT PRESS?

Student newspapers bear some strange names such as *Grass High, Pflashlyte,* and the *Brown Watermelon.* Controversy has arisen in settings which involve both the literary contents of these efforts and the sale or distribution of the paper on the school campus. In *Scoville v. Board of Education of Joliet Township School District* (286 F. Supp. 988, 1968) the writing and distribution of *Grass High* was upheld and the court indicated that the use of pornographic materials was an adolescent attempt to shock elders. Frequent cases have arisen in this area. Administrators are inclined to discipline severely students who, through their writing, attack, and advocate disobedience to, school rules and regulations, defame school administrators or principals, and use excessively four-letter words often referred to as filthy, suggestive, or pornographic. Several of the cases in this area have advocated successfully that expulsion orders based upon a student's exercise of rights of free speech and press were an exercise of authority in excess of that delegated to the local school board by the state.

The general pattern utilized by school administrators to deal with the student underground press has been to subject the students to rules requiring them to submit a copy to the administration for approval before the publication can be circulated on the school campus. When confronted with this issue the courts have drawn some distinction between "speech" and "speech-connected" activities. School authorities may reasonably regulate in carefully restricted situations speech-connected activities. One such incident involved the distribution of leaflets attempting to solicit monetary support for the support of the legal defense of the "Chicago Seven." The school had a rule of long standing which prohibited the solicitation of funds on the school grounds because numerous solicitors in the past had successfully persuaded school children to give their lunch money to various causes. The school only had to show that the rule reasonably related to the successful operation of the public school. Where "pure speech" is involved the burden of proof requires a showing a "compelling state interest" to justify prior restraint.

Judicial authorities repeatedly emphasize that they expect the schools to nurture and protect constitutional rights and extinguish them only where they can find no practical alternative to regulation. The court will intervene only in that area of discretion where school authorities go beyond the area where reasonable minds may differ. Emphasis has also been given to the necessity for the existence of some buttressing facts justifying such action as contrasted to some dire prediction or anticipation of difficulty.

Where the school attempts to require prior approval of the student's speech or speech-related activities, its rules must comply with the requirements imposed by the court in *Butts* v. *Dallas*

Independent School District (436 F 2d. 728, rev. 306 F. Supp. 488, 1969), which include:

1. Expeditious review procedure.
2. Specify to whom and how material may be submitted for clearance.
3. Type of publication allowed.
4. Kinds of disruption which justify censorship.

Special care has to be given to regulations being framed in this area because of the problems which are inherent in over-broad rules. The key to constitutionality in this entire area appears to be what constitutes a material disruption to the educational environment. Where the school program is disrupted the right to regulate generally follows because this appears to be one of the basic concerns of the state—a school program continuing without undue disruptive influences at work. It appears that the court is more concerned about the greater risk of suppressing free speech and press among the young than in regulating the abuse of free speech and press by the few.

FREEDOM OF ASSOCIATION AND THE SCHOOLS

The freedom guaranteed in the First Amendment in connection with the right of the people to peaceably assemble remains largely an abstract concept in a school setting. Many states have long had statutes controlling membership and participation in certain kinds of organizations. With a few exceptions, the statutes which prohibit fraternities, sororities, and secret societies have generally been upheld. The courts have had little difficulty distinguishing between the rights of adults in society at large, where attempts to control their association would obviously be unconstitutional, and students in a compulsory educational environment, where such organizations would detrimentally affect student morale in addition to being undemocratic. The constitutionality of these statutes has twice gone to the Supreme Court and they have been upheld each time. Picketing and parading on public school premises may be regulated in maintaining an efficient system of public schools. Although the right to assemble and to speak or to hear speakers may be related to the guarantees of the First Amendment, the demand for an orderly school environment may supersede the individual right to speak or to hear a speaker. It had been suggested that children in a school are a captive audience—compelled by law to be there—and are not possessed of that full capacity for free choice that forms the presupposition of the First Amendment guarantees. Where students tested school regulations which prohibited activities such as "singing and marching down the hallways during school hours" and attempting to conduct a speech-related rally with "abrasive and contemptuous behavior," the courts refused to interfere with the discretionary use of school authority. Neither was a 300-student sit-in outside a school principal's office protesting the suspension of three other students determined to be within the protected freedoms. At best, the attempts by judicial authorities to define or test the limits of the right of students to assemble have resulted in few insights for the use of either students or school professionals. The uppermost concern of both court and school administrators to this point seems to be the maintenance of a disruption-free educational environment.

THE SCHOOLS AND THE FOURTH AMENDMENT

A considerable amount of litigation has arisen in a public school setting involving the "unreasonable search and seizure" phrase of the Fourth Amendment. Most of the cases in this area have surrounded either the search of the student or the locker that he utilized at school for his books or other personal belongings. The object of the search in most of the cases involved was some contraband item usually possessed by the student in violation of law. Numerous cases have involved marijuana or some other drug that is subject to control statutes, while others have involved stolen property sought as evidence for a non-school related crime. It has long been assumed by school personnel that they had the right to search school lockers or to require the student to empty his pockets before a principal or other school administrator. Recent litigation, while bringing such acts into question, has found the courts generally supportive of such practices by utilizing the doctrine of "in loco parentis" or by arriving at the conclusion that such search did not meet the standard of unreasonableness as prohibited by the Fourth Amendment.

Two California cases, *In re Donaldson* (75 Cal. Rptr. 220, 1969) and *In re G* (90 Cal. Rptr. 361, 1970), illustrate the problem. In the first case, a vice principal searched a fifteen-year-old student's locker, where he found cigarettes made of marijuana and a plastic bag containing marijuana. In the second case the principal, acting without a warrant, required a student to empty his pockets because of information he had gained from another student and his intoxicated behavior. In both cases the court ruled that there had been no violation of the Fourth Amendment. The cases become a little more clouded when the search of student lockers is carried out by police officers or detectives with the consent of the school official. In two cases where this condition existed, *People* v. *Overton* (20 N.Y.S 2d 360, 1967) and *State* v. *Stein* (456 P. 2d 1, 1969), the police were allowed to search without a search warrant but in the second case the student agreed to the search. More recent cases tend to strengthen the positions taken in the earlier decisions. Two lines of thought have developed in this area. The first emphasizes the fact that while a student has control of his locker as against other students that such is not the case with school officials. It is deemed proper and appropriate that school authorities inspect them as to their proper use. Such inspection is held to be an inherent right vested in school administrators. The second line of reasoning which supports such searches is that a school principal stands "in loco parentis" for disciplinary purposes and that a "reasonable suspicion" is sufficient cause for a search, and since he acts with the nature of a private person, not in concert with the police, the Fourth Amendment prohibition is not applicable. Search does not appear to be much of a problem to public school administrators when there is reasonable suspicion of a student's activities.

DUE PROCESS AND EQUAL PROTECTION UNDER THE FIFTH AND FOURTEENTH AMENDMENTS

As late as 1959 courts were extremely reluctant to assume jurisdiction in cases which raised the issues of due process or equal protection in most educational settings. The "due process" problem was complicated by a judicial doctrine of long standing which took the position that society extended a "privilege" to a student when it provided him with a tax-supported education. If attendance at a public school or university was so classified the state could deprive an individual of that opportunity without meeting a constitutional issue. In the *Dixon Case* (186 F. Supp. 945, 1960) the court reinterpreted this doctrine to indicate that education had now become such a fundamental need that it should be considered as a "substantial right." The court added, "whenever a governmental body acts so as to injure an individual," the constitution requires that the act be consonant with due process of law. The "due process" concept has developed into two types of considerations, that is, procedural and substantive. Since there have been so many cases in this area, only an outline of the various decisions is necessary to get the idea of each doctrine across.

It should be remembered that when any governmental body acts to deprive any citizen of a substantial right it must comport with due process of law. In a procedural sense this means that the following steps should be taken before a student is expelled from a public institution:

1. Rules governing student behavior should be circulated to the students and their parents at the opening of school.
2. A notice should be given to the student in writing stating with some particularity the charges which have been lodged against him.
3. The notice should be timely and give sufficient time for the individual to prepare a defense.
4. A fair hearing should be held which includes:
   a. Availability to the accused of affidavits or other evidence against him.
   b. Use of counsel if he desires.
   c. In the absence of compelling reasons for not doing so, permitting the cross-examination of witnesses.
   d. Permitting the accused the right of introducing evidence in his own behalf.
   e. A transcript should be made available.
5. A finding should be submitted within a reasonable time which states those charges found to be true and the decisions of the disciplinary body, and
6. The individual should be informed as to his right of appeal.

The second phase of this doctrine has involved the notion called "substantive due process." As a general standard the courts have said that the entire procedure should be "fundamentally fair." Among the issues that have been resolved in this area have been:

1. Rules by which students are to be governed should not be unduly vague.
2. Students should not be disciplined on the basis of unwritten rules.
3. Decisions should be supported with findings of substantial evidence.
4. The identity of principal witnesses should be revealed.

5. Student is entitled to a hearing before an impartial tribunal, and

6. A public or private hearing on the request of the accused.

The student has the right to an education so that he is entitled to fair, impartial, and considerate treatment from the school or college.

EQUAL PROTECTION IN THE SCHOOL SETTING

Two areas of decision in regard to this constitutional protection have brought about and will continue for some time to bring about the most profound changes experienced in American education in the past century. The first decision was that of *Brown* v. *Board of Education* (347 U.S. 483, 1954), which announced a new educational philosophy in public education. For more than a half century the U.S. Supreme Court had followed the doctrine of "separate but equal" facilities as not being repugnant to the equal protection clause. In that historic decision the Court departed from its prior decisions and declared that when a facility was set apart by statute to be attended by one race it was inherently unequal to attend it. The impact of the initial decision and federal action primarily was focused on the states which had maintained "de jure" segregation, or segregation by state law. Its full impact upon public schools will continue to be felt for some time to come as efforts are brought to bear upon the "de facto" segregation, or that segregation which is brought about by economic, housing, or other factors. It will probably be many years before all of the progeny of the *Brown Case* are out of the courts and the last court order is implemented.

The second type of decision under the banner of equal protection has been those which have questioned the financial system of the public schools. The various state statutes which govern the distribution of funds for the development of local educational programs result in greatly disparate expenditure of public funds. It is obvious from only a cursory examination of statistics on per capita expenditures that the effort and ability of local districts have little to do with the amounts expended to support the educational program. The first generation of court suits in this area is characterized by *Hobson* v. *Hansen* (269 F. Supp. 401, 1967), which questioned intra-district differences in per pupil expenditures. The second generation cases in this line follow the reasoning found in *Serranto* v. *Priest* (487 P. 2d 1241, 1971), which attacked the differences in expenditure on an inter-district basis. Other cases in this line will be discussed in a later chapter. Suffice it to say, that some type of equalized expenditure is likely to be the outcome of these cases, which in effect will narrow the differences in local school districts to support an educational program.

A RIGHT TO PRIVACY—FOURTH OR NINTH AMENDMENT!

In a somewhat recent case, *Griswold* v. *Connecticut* (381 U.S. 479, 1965), a "fundamental right" was discovered which was used by the U.S. Supreme Court to strike down an anti-contraceptive information law. The amendment reads:

> The enumeration in the constitution, of certain rights, shall not be construed to deny or disparge others retained by the people.

Privacy as spelled out in *Griswold* is not specified in the U.S. Constitution but apparently is some type of sub-right which persons concerned with individual rights have been trying to get recognized for about a half century. Students who were interested in the personal rights associated with dress and grooming attempted to take advantage of the preceding decision to get another freedom established. The effort, *Davis* v. *Firment* (269 F. Supp. 524, 1967), failed when the court held that the issue of grooming was not a "fundamental" enough interest to classify it as a protected right. In subsequent cases the federal Circuit Courts of Appeals have split on this issue. The federal courts have been clogged with cases of this type for several years with as many as fifty cases appearing in an eighteen-month period. The U.S. Supreme Court could have settled the issue in a case styled *Breen* v. *Kahl* (419 F. 2d 1034, 1969), which had upheld a student's choice of hair length as a personal freedom protected by the First, Ninth, and Fourteenth Amendments, but the Court declined to hear it on a Writ of Certiorari. The last word has not been heard in this area.

SUMMARY

Interestingly, a number of recent publications have paralleled the rights of students with a statement of responsibilities. The Connecticut Education Association has published a statement under the heading of "atmosphere" in which students are said to have the "right to learn, free from arbitrary restrictions," and the corresponding responsibility to "utilize the learning process effectively and to take maximum advantage of educational opportunity, with respect for the teacher as an individual person." The Newton, Massachusetts, public schools have also published a set of guidelines. The publication declares, "We recognize the student's right to freedom of speech, freedom of press, to peaceful assembly and to petition for the correction of grievances," but "accompanying responsibilities flow from the exercise of these rights." Among the values listed are:

Respect for one's self.
Respect for others and their rights.
Respect for individual dignity.
Respect for legally constituted authority.

Although some would like to return to the good old days, one must wonder whether they were really very good. Certainly these decisions on the exercise of personal rights must produce a generation of adults who are far more sensitive to individual needs of citizens to participate in the processes of government and education.

SELECTED BIBLIOGRAPHY

Books

ALEXANDER, KERN, RAY CORNS, and WALTER McCANN. *Public School Law.* St. Paul, Minn.: West Publishing Co., 1969. 734 pages. This text was written as cases and materials suitable for a course in a professional school of law or education, but Chapter 3, "Religion and the Public School," is a well conceived unit and the cases represent well the law in the area.

BOLMEIER, E. C. *Legal Limits of Authority over the Pupil.* Charlottesville, Va.: The Michie Co., 1970. 150 pages. A well written, easily understood piece of legal literature. It will go out of date somewhat rapidly, however, because the author has a tendency to capitalize on one or two leading cases, which may be overturned with some rapidity.

FLOWERS, ANNE, and EDWARD C. BOLMEIER. *Law and Pupil Control.* Cincinnati: W. H. Anderson Co., 1964. 194 pages. This reference is a short, well written text but it is suspect in many of its conclusions because of the recent decisions of courts in several areas such as married students participating in co-curricular activities. Recent cases should be added to the commentary of the book before full acceptance is given.

National Organization on Legal Problems in Education. *Emerging Problems in School Law.* Topeka, Kan.: N.O.L.P.E., 1972. 205 pages. Two papers presented at the 1971 meeting of N.O.L.P.E. contribute significant insights into the relationships between courts and student rights. The twin doctrines of procedural and substantive matters concerning student rights are well developed and documented.

Periodicals and Pamphlets

ABBOTT, C. MICHAEL. "The Student Press: Some First Impressions." *Wayne Law Review.* 16:1 (Winter 1969). A well written analysis of the impact of unsanctioned newspapers that have appeared on high school and college campuses. The author indicates that students have for too long been denied their say and that their present insistence appears non-negotiable.

American Council on Education. *A Judicial Document on Student Discipline.* (Printed in *Educational Record,* Winter 1969.) Washington, D.C.: American Council on Education, 1968. 9 pages. An unusual order issued by the Federal District Court of the Western District of Missouri which reviews the relationships between students, faculty, and administration of institutions of higher education which are tax-supported.

BAKKEN, CLARENCE J. "Student Rights as Seen by a Lawyer-Educator." *Journal of College Student Personnel.* 6:136 (March 1965). One of the early articles suggesting that college personnel in the area of admissions and personnel services should take a hard look at the developing law of student rights. A contrast is provided between the concepts of education as operated for the benefit of society and education for the benefit of the individual.

KATZ, JOSEPH, and NEVITT SANFORD. "The New Student Power and Needed Educational Reform." *Phi Delta Kappan.* 47:397 (April 1966). An article oriented to the concept of power in which the authors see students joining the traditional estates of faculty, administration, and trustees in shaping the school and college experience. In the demise of the doctrine of "in loco parentis" the authors see a new opportunity to force students to make their own decisions and assume a greater share of the responsibility for their own behavior.

LANGER, JOHN H. *School-Law Enforcement Cooperation.* (Mimeograph.) Dallas, Texas: Southern Methodist University School of Law, 1970. 7 pages. A thought-provoking article reflecting upon the responsibility of school administrators to enforce laws in regard to drug abuse on school campuses. The author encourages school discipline independent of local law enforcement agencies but questions the right of the school not to prosecute under criminal statutes where appropriate.

National School Public Relations Association. *Student Rights and Responsibilities, Courts Force Schools to Change.* Washington, D.C.: National School Public Relations Association, 1972. 64 pages. A well rounded publication which voices both the views of students and educators in connection with student rights and responsibilities with sample statements of local school policies, dress codes, and student Bill of Rights review.

SHANNON, THOMAS A. *The Developing Civil Rights of Students in the Public Elementary and Secondary Schools in the 1970's.* San Diego, Calif.: San Diego City Schools, 1971. 8 pages. A short treatise by a practicing school attorney in connection with which school personnel are urged to recognize the developing rights of students. The author feels that a continued disregard of legal trends will foster and extend internal conflict in the school environment.

University Council for Educational Administration. *Educational Administration Quarterly.* Columbus, Ohio: E. A. Publications. Vol. 7, No. 3 (Autumn 1971). An excellent discussion of the issues in connection with the disruptive student is found in the lead article, "Toward an Educationally Appropriate Definition of Disruptive Student Behavior," written by Edward T. Ladd. His treatment of the educational potential of disruptive behavior is particularly stimulating.

CHAPTER 8

School Finance and Equal Protection

Financial support for the public schools has primarily been a blending of state and local efforts. Federal support has been designed by the Congress to encourage development in special program areas or to remedy certain problems which were perceived as being in the national interest. As a result the per pupil expenditures for public education have varied tremendously from state to state, or even within a state, because of the wide disparities in ability and willingness to support educational programs. The history of state support for educational programs is difficult to document before the latter quarter of the 1800s even though some support was evident, especially at the elementary level, because several state constitutions provided such support. Tax-supported secondary schools developed quite rapidly during the fourth quarter of the nineteenth century. Federal participation prior to 1900 had been quite limited outside the land grants or other special incentives provided by federal legislation.

The modern era in school administration with emphasis on school finance was generated after the turn of the twentieth century. Men such as Ellwood P. Cubberley, George D. Strayer, Sr., Paul R. Mort, and Henry C. Morrison shaped the basic theory of financial support which would tend to equalize educational support and educational opportunity at the state level. The various state legislatures were slow in accepting the tax burden thrust upon them by a recognition of the Tenth Amendment responsibility for educational support. Even when sophisticated financial programs developed they were primarily of a foundation program philosophy which emphasized local effort and management, providing a statewide minimum expenditure. The level of local expenditure became a function of local property value and a willingness of local patrons to tax themselves to provide a desired level of enrichment. The predominant source of tax support continued to be at the local level even though the level of state and federal support has greatly increased.

Most local school districts are limited to the property tax to generate local revenue. The burden of local taxes for school purposes falls upon the real property owner and as this burden has increased the discrepancy in expenditure between districts with large assessed valuations and those with low assessed valuations has increased. These patterns have also been reflected between the states with high and low ability to tax themselves as represented by income per capita. In many cases these high- and low-ability districts might be geographically adjacent to one another. The difference in ability would be based upon the development of some major industrial installation or the discovery of mineral wealth which would greatly increase the assessed valuation for local property tax purposes. In many cases districts with limited property values were willing to assess higher taxes than the more wealthy districts and would still have fewer resources with which to support a local educational program. Since the "educational industry" at the public school level now employs over three million persons and has an annual budget of approximately forty billion dollars, more and more attention is being devoted to its problems.

DIFFERENCES IN INTRA-DISTRICT EXPENDITURES

Litigation over school expenditures, viewing them through a philosophical framework related to "equal protection" of the law, is a comparatively recent phenomenon. Although many school administrators were aware of differentials in expenditure both on an intra-district and inter-district basis, little had been done to correct these problems. The same could be said about differences in expenditure between states. Much debate had gone on in the Congress concerning the problem, and bills were introduced to remedy the problem but they always seemed to founder on issues such as federal control.

The issue was finally joined at the local level in a suit which was filed in Washington, D.C., styled *Hobson* v. *Hansen* (269 F. Supp. 401, 1967). This case was essentially a case which sought to enforce the *Brown* and *Bolling* decisions in the Washington, D.C., schools. It achieved a great deal of publicity because the court declared the much publicized "track" system of curriculum design as being both undemocratic and discriminatory. One of the less publicized findings was that there had been a $100 per pupil difference in expenditure between predominantly Negro elementary schools ($292.00) and the predominantly white elementary schools ($392.00). This differential in expenditure was brought about by teacher assignment policies which gave preference to assignment requests for teachers with more lengthy periods of service with the district. On a second hearing of this case, the court ordered an equalization of expenditure within the district and announced that he would only tolerate 5 percent variation between schools. Other decisions had declared that the state must administer its educational function in all parts of the state with an open hand such as in *Griffin* v. *School Board* (377 U.S. 218, 1964). The courts in most of the cases did not venture into per pupil expenditures on an intra-district basis. They usually satisfied themselves with instructions that education was the most important function of the state and that it had an obligation to provide equal protection for its citizens as a constitutional command.

DIFFERENCES IN INTER-DISTRICT EXPENDITURES

Many of the first court cases which were to test differences in local school expenditures under state equalization formulas were generally brought by disgruntled taxpayers who were seeking relief under equality and uniformity of taxation provisions found in many state constitutions. In most of the cases the complainant did not have in mind the equalization of educational opportunity but was seeking some means of redress for his own tax problems. In a number of these cases the taxpayer was not concerned with greater or more equitable distribution of state funds, but was seeking to find some limitation to the existing method which saw a local district as paying out more taxes to the state than it was receiving in return. Most of these cases were treated by the courts under precedents involving taxation, and the equalization schemes were conceived in such a way as to be justified as reasonable classifications when attacked with a Fourteenth Amendment argument. Variations in support and expenditure could easily be related to some justifiable circumstance which existed in schools or communities with certain characteristics.

The identification of education in the *Brown* decision as one of the fundamental interests of our society which must be made available to all its children on equal terms has brought about a renewed interest in making application of the equal protection clause to school district expenditures. In *Reynolds* v. *Sims* (377 U.S. 533, 1964) the U.S. Supreme Court indicated that the "equal protection" clause requires the uniform treatment of persons standing in the same relation to governmental action. Subsequent court decisions relating to state school finance laws have brought about a series of decisions which promise to bring about widespread changes in the school support patterns.

The first and most widely known of these decisions was the *Serrano v. Priest* (96 Cal. Rptr. 601, 1971) in California and has since been utilized as a pattern for a flood of cases filed in other states. The case was brought as a class action by a group of elementary and high school pupils and their parents against the state and county officials concerned with the financing of public schools, asking for a declaratory judgment that the school financing scheme was unconstitutional and asking for injunctive relief. The California scheme was heavily dependent upon local property taxes, and variations in the wealth of a local district brought about wide disparities in local district expenditures. In a far-reaching decision the court made a finding that the scheme was invidiously discriminatory against the poor because it makes the quality of a child's education a function of the wealth of his parents and his neighbors. The court further in the opinion stated, "Recognizing as we must that the right to an education in our public schools is a fundamental interest which cannot be conditioned upon wealth, we can discern no compelling state purpose necessitating the present method of financing." They concluded their opinion with a finding that "such a system cannot withstand constitutional challenge and must fall before the equal protection clause."

The complaint in this case alleges wide disparities in accessibility to funds and to actual expenditures of educational dollars. The facts brought out in the case supported such findings. The abilities are cited in the table.

The tax bases alone yield differences of the order of 10,000 to one in the abilities to support the local educational program. Although the state's efforts at equalization and supplemental aid do tend to temper the disparities which result from the wide variation in property values, the wide differentials in ability still remain and result in broad differences in expenditure.

Since education is a fundamental interest, the court applied a standard which required the state to meet the burden of establishing a compelling interest which justifies the California school finance law. The court noted that the differences which exist are brought about primarily by the uneven distribution of commercial and industrial properties in the state. Such variability in ability and tax effort presents problems which deny equal education opportunity and local tax equity. When the final outcomes of this case can be evaluated it is likely that its influence will rival that of *Brown* v. *Board of Education*, since each state except Hawaii has a similar method of financing public schools.

ASSESSED VALUATIONS PER PUPIL
1969-1970

	ELEMENTARY	HIGH SCHOOL
Low	$ 103.00	$ 11,959.00
Median	19,600.00	41,300.00
High	952,156.00	349,093.00

PER PUPIL EXPENDITURES
1969-1970

	ELEMENTARY	HIGH SCHOOL	UNIFIED
Low	$ 407.00	$ 722.00	$ 612.00
Median	672.00	898.00	766.00
High	2,586.00	1,767.00	2,414.00

Two other cases of similar importance were decided by federal district courts in Minnesota and in Texas. The Minnesota case, *Van Dusartz* v. *Hatfield* (334 F. Supp. 870, 1971), followed the ruling of the *Serrano* case and ruled that the child's education may not be a function of the wealth of a local district but must be a function of the wealth of the state as a whole. The court also disposed of rather summarily the argument that there was no relationship between cost and quality. It stated:

> While the correlation between expenditure per pupil and the quality of education may be open to argument, the Court must assume that it is high. To do otherwise would be to hold that in these wealthy districts where the per pupil expenditure is higher than some real or imaginary norm, the school boards are merely wasting the taxpayer's money. The Court is not willing to so hold, absent some strong evidence.

When legislators and school administrators are constantly calling for increased state and local tax support it seems a bit strange that educators would submit the issue to the court that there is no relationship between cost and quality when it is assumed to bear some relationship in most other economic activities.

The *Rodriguez* v. *San Antonio Independent School District* (Civil Action No. 68-175-SA, W.D. of Texas) was another case of this type. Each school district in Texas is authorized to levy local property taxes to meet its share of the cost of the Foundation School Program, to finance capital outlay for buildings, and for costs above the minimum program. The court recognized that the system assumes that the assessed valuation of property within the various districts would be sufficiently equal to sustain comparable expenditures from one district to another. In short, the court again found that education was made a function of the local property tax base. In seeking a solution for this situation the plaintiffs advocated a principle of "fiscal neutrality" which would make the wealth of the entire state become the determinant of the quality of the educational program. After examining data which indicated that the wealthier districts were enabled to spend more per pupil while paying less taxes than the poorer districts could spend while paying more taxes, the court found as a matter of law that plaintiffs had been denied equal protection of the law which was guaranteed by the Fourteenth Amendment. The state education authority and the state legislature were given two years to restructure the allocation of school finances so that education will become a function of the wealth of the state as a whole. Although later overturned by the United States Supreme Court, *Rodriguez* is still likely to have a strong influence on school finance.

The court in this case studiously avoided, as did the plaintiffs, any advocacy that the expenditures per pupil be equal. It did recognize that some judicially manageable standard seemed imperative but rejected the notion of educational need that had been advocated in *McInnis* v. *Shapire* (293 F. Supp. 327, 1968). The court felt that such a nebulous concept would have involved the court in fruitless research and evaluation. It similarly rejected a concept of "varying needs" which had been urged upon the court in *Burrus* v. *Wilkerson* (310 F. Supp. 572, 1969). The court refused both of these ideas as unworkable standards and established the "fiscal neutrality" as the basis of any new scheme of school finance for the state. Numerous other cases of this type have been filed throughout the United States. An educated guess at this stage would seem to indicate that far-reaching changes in the public school financing systems in most states will occur to meet the challenge of "equal protection" within the state's educational program.

These decisions necessarily bring into question the conditions within the state which will meet the equal protection standard. While an equal expenditure per pupil would satisfy this standard simplistically, any practicing school administrator would have to acknowledge that such an approach would not in fact equalize educational opportunity. In other desegregation cases, decisions have been made which justified additional expenditures where it was necessary to remedy past inequities. The Congress also built such features into the Economic Opportunity Act (42 U.S.C. Sects. 2781-2791) and the Elementary and Secondary Education Act (20 U.S.C. Sects. 241a-411) to meet the special needs of disadvantaged schools. Differentials in costs between programs such as elementary and secondary schools, liberal arts and occupational programs, rural and urban schools, normal and exceptional children, and schools requiring transportation as contrasted to those which do not will have to be written into any new law. If such considerations are not built into a new statutory scheme the inequalities which would result would be as great as those which the court sought to remedy. Simplistic solutions, however appealing they seem, simply will not equalize educational opportunity. Some authorities indicate that the real culprit in the situation is not equalized expenditure but equalized access to the funds necessary for a quality program for all children.

INTERSTATE DIFFERENCES IN EDUCATIONAL EXPENDITURES

If anyone examines the expenditures per pupil in average daily attendance among the states he will be surprised at the differences between states. A recent issue of *Rankings Among the States, 1971* (Washington, D.C.: Research Division, National Education Association, 1971) indicates that there is a wide variation of expenditures which bears a high correlation to the net income per child in average daily attendance. The expenditure levels between states show as much variation as do those between districts. It is logical to assume that the "equal protection" doctrine could have a wide application to these differences. Although school support could be argued to be a state rather than a federal responsibility, it seems that a political as well as legal perspective would demand some kind of equalization of opportunity between states.

School finance studies generally show that delegation of taxing authority to smaller units of government creates differences in fiscal capacity. The smaller the units created and the greater the taxing authority which is granted to them, the more difference will result. It is highly likely that a case similar to those already mentioned at the state level will be filed, attempting to equalize expenditures between states. This has traditionally been a troublesome issue in the courts; however, the more recent interpretation of the "general welfare" clause would permit more effective participation in this field. Federal assistance has been bogged down in the federal Congress in many sessions by the debate between categorical aids and general support for the public schools. Categorical aids have multiplied during this period of debate primarily because of the distrust of the concentration of governmental power and influence. Meanwhile the shocking differences in level of education and educational expenditures have continued.

Numerous plans for federal participation in the costs of public schools have been suggested. All appear to be based on the notion that about the same amount per pupil should be expended in each state. One approach that has been suggested is that of a minimum foundation program in which the federal government would allocate funds on the basis of the state's ability to support education to meet some minimum expenditure. A second approach that has been suggested is that of an equal grant per pupil without any monitoring of state or local effort. Although this would reduce the ratios of funds available for education in the richest and poorest states, it would not equalize the expenditure. Since the states would start with unequal amounts, the funds available would still show great variation, although at a higher range. Others have argued incentive plans whereby the federal grants would be allotted according to the state's ability to support education. Theorists have suggested that Congress should require the states to levy a tax equal to a certain percentage of net income before they would receive a maximum federal grant. This approach runs contrary to the plans for highway and other types of support where the state receives a fixed percentage of what it is willing to spend. The maximum local effort requirement for a jointly supported program appears to be sound.

While the arguments continue in political circles, the schools continue to operate with disparate levels of financial support. If the executive branch cannot provide sufficient leadership to overcome public inertia and the legislative branch cannot find a formula for support which is politically acceptable, it remains for the judicial branch to provide the needed incentive for action in this area. Such action will probably be forthcoming even though *Rodriguez* did not survive arguments before the Supreme Court. "Equal protection" between states should be the same standard that has been applied to the individual districts as in *Hobson* or the differences within a state between districts as in *Serrano*.

SUMMARY

The courts in which the school finance cases have been argued have studiously avoided identifying programs of finance which appear to meet the "equal protection" test. It is apparent that school men will be confronted with the language of these cases for sometime to come. Constitutional standards such as "the wealth being dependent upon the total wealth of the state" will probably be expanded to cover the entire country as a base. Each state legislature will have to concern itself with whether or not "each child has an equal access to educational programs as well as equal access to dollars." Some attention will also have to be given to "educational need," which the courts tend to avoid as being a non-justiciable standard, because children with a typical need are more expensive than children in regular programs. The courts will have to continue to function in this area because the executive and legislative branches have not been able to perform well in this area of leadership and recognition of constitutional standards.

SELECTED BIBLIOGRAPHY

Books

American Association of School Administrators. *The Federal Government and the Public Schools*. Washington, D.C.: American Association of School Administrators, 1965. 70 pages. Although this booklet is almost ten years old, it has an interesting concluding chapter which forecasts a federal-state-local partnership in financing schools.

GAUERKE, WARREN E., and JACK R. CHILDRESS, eds. *The Theory and Practices of School Finance*. Chicago: Rand McNally, 1967. 563 pages. A recent text dealing with many of the current issues in school finance. It contains several excellent chapters dealing with issues concerning school inputs and productivity.

JOHNS, ROE L., KERN ALEXANDER, and K. FORBIS JORDAN, eds. *Financing Education, Fiscal and Legal Alternatives*. Columbus, Ohio: Charles E. Merrill, 1972. 508 pages. This recent book is the product of the National Educational Finance Project and provides a sophisticated look at the school finance problem. The beginning student in professional education will find that he must acquire some new vocabulary before he can pursue it with understanding.

PETERSON, LEROY J. *Yearbook of School Law, 1972.* Topeka, Kan.: National Organization on Legal Problems in Education, 1972. 260 pages. An excellent discussion of the *Serrano* and *Rodriguez* cases are found in Chapter 4 which is an excellent discussion of the most recent decisions dealing with school finance issues.

SHANNON, THOMAS A., et al. *Emerging Problems in School Law.* Topeka, Kan.: National Organization on Legal Problems in Education, 1972. 205 pages. An interesting paper given at the annual meeting of the N.O.L.P.E. at Los Vegas is entitled "After Serrano" and is included in this volume as one contribution.

Periodicals

Case Note. "Development in the Law—Equal Protection." 82 *Harvard Law Review* 1065, 1129 (1969). A discussion of the pivotal role of education in American culture and the fact that it is essential to opening up to the individual the central experiences of our culture. The value of such education being undeniable lends application to the "equal protection" standard.

COONS, JOHN E., WILLIAM H. CLINE III, and STEPHEN D. SUGARMAN. "Educational Opportunity: A Workable Constitutional Test for State Financial Structures." 57 *California Law Review* 305-15 (1969). This is an article widely quoted in the *Serrano* v. *Priest* case as to the importance of education to society as we know it. It contains a compelling argument as to the importance of the public schools, particularly to the children of the poor, in rescuing certain children from a culturally and socially depressed society.

HOROWITZ, HAROLD W., and DIANA L. NEITRING, "Equal Protection Aspects of Inequalities in Public Education and Public Assistance Programs from Place to Place Within a State." 15 *U.C.L.A. Law Review* 787, 806 (1968). An analysis of the district's ability to share in educational costs, since it is limited to the property tax as a source of revenue. Variations in assessed valuation and tax effort bring on both tax inequity and deny equal protection of the law.

KURLAND, PHILIP B. "Equal Educational Opportunity: The Limits of Constitutional Jurisprudence Undefined." 36 *University of Chicago Law Review* 583-85 (1968). An analysis of cases which have dealt with apportionment in which the courts have refused to recognize discrimination among citizens even if it is caused by accidents of geography or boundary line of local government.

NEWHOUSE, WADE J. *Constitutional Uniformity and Equality in State Taxation.* Ann Arbor: University of Michigan Law School, 1959. Pp. 602-03. A discussion of the additional limitations which the "equal protection" clause imposes over that of state constitutions, such as a minimum standard of uniformity.

CHAPTER 9

The Teacher and Liability for Pupil Injury

One of the growing areas of special concern to professional educators has been that of possible liability for an injury which occurs to a pupil while the educator participates in some aspect of the pupil management system of the public schools. Judgments have been rendered in trial courts in which the plaintiff has received a judgment as high as four million dollars. Under our system of law each individual has the right of inviolacy of his person. He enjoys the right to be free from bodily injury whether intentionally or carelessly caused by others. It is a basic concept or doctrine of the common law that every individual should be liable for his own torts or wrongful acts, whether such acts are intentional or the result of negligence. Most of the suits which are filed against school personnel allege negligence on the part of an individual resulting in injury to a pupil. Since all school personnel are susceptible to suit for alleged negligence, professional employees should perform with a high degree of care to prevent school accidents and protect pupils from injury. It should be remembered that the teacher is not automatically liable for a pupil injury; the liability arises when negligence on the part of the teacher is the causative factor in the injury.

A LEGAL DEFINITION OF NEGLIGENCE

The legal test of a tortious act which may result in a judgment for damages involves at least four elements: (1) the existence of a legal duty of one person to another, (2) a breach of the duty existing between the two parties, (3) the breach of duty must be the proximate cause of the injury to the damaged party, and (4) a result involving monetary damages. Such a breach may arise in one of three ways:

1. Misfeasance—the defendant was acting but in an improper manner. The individual charged with negligent behavior acts exhibiting a proper motive but acts imprudently. A recent case where a classroom teacher, when momentarily distracted, scalded the hand of a child she was attempting to assist by washing out a wound would be a good illustration of such an act. The teacher was acting with the proper motive but acted with little wisdom.
2. Nonfeasance—the defendant failed to act when he had a duty to do so. Many of the cases involving nonfeasance result from a teacher being away from his place of assigned responsibility when an accident or injury occurs.
3. Malfeasance—the defendant acts but in a situation where he exhibits a bad motive or inflicts a deliberate injury. A recent case involving a coach is illustrative of this problem. A student attempted to assault the coach, who reacted by knocking the attacking student to the gym floor. While the student was lying on the floor the coach dropped on his abdomen with his knee, causing a severe injury. He had a right to use such force as was necessary to repel the attack on his person. Once the student was on the gym floor the act bringing about the injury was not justified and the resulting court decision was that such act was deliberately intended to injure the student.

This concept called negligence also has within it some notion of foreseeability and requires the educator to perform as a reasonably prudent person of similar training and circumstance should perform. This "reasonable, prudent person" is a variable standard and requires the teacher to perform on a standard equivalent to his training, age, experience, maturity, and other related characteristics. A California case, *Pirkle* v. *Oakdale Union Grammar School District* (253 P. 2d 1, 1953), defined the standard of care required as follows: "The standard of care required of an officer or employee of a public school is that which a person of ordinary prudence charged with his duties, would exercise under the same circumstances." Negligence then devolves into two basic circumstances: (1) an act which a reasonable, prudent man should have realized involved an unreasonable risk of injury to other persons and (2) the failure to perform an act properly which a person undertakes to do, or the failure to perform at all a duty necessary to protect the plaintiff which he was under a legal duty to transact, or he may have acted deliberately to injure the plaintiff. In either of the cases an actual damage must occur in which a monetary loss is suffered. A person may perform as negligently as he wishes so long as he does not damage another person.

Not all accidents in which pupils are injured result in teacher liability. Depending on the state where the accident occurs, a plea of unavoidable accident may be used as a defense. In other states a comparative degree of negligence may be used to defeat part of the recovery where the injured person also exhibited some negligence. In other states the plaintiff must be found to be completely free of negligence or it will defeat his recovery. Some accidents are going to occur even though a teacher has taken precautions against them. In a case styled *Gaincott* v. *Davis* (275 N.W. 229, 1937) a teacher permitted a child to use a milk bottle to water a plant growing in the classroom. The child used a chair to reach the pot, which was hanging from the ceiling. In the process the child fell from the chair, broke the bottle, and was severely cut. The teacher was not held liable. The court felt that the fall and cut were not within the normal scope of foreseeability. Some authorities feel that this case was not well decided; nevertheless, it illustrates the fact that there must be a finding of legal negligence before there can be a recovery against the professional person.

WHAT STANDARD OF CARE DOES THE TEACHER OWE TO THE PUPIL?

The standard applied to most cases is that of the reasonable prudent man who is said to be in the same or similar circumstances. This is a fictional standard which should influence the standard of behavior of the defendant in this kind of case. The standard is applied by the jury and is considered a fact issue. It seems reasonable to hold a teacher to the standard of behavior which he holds out to the public. When he considered himself to be a master teacher and holds himself out to the public as such it seems equitable to require the individual practitioner to perform at that professional level. This "reasonable prudent man" concept also has as a part of the notion a characteristic referred to in legal literature as foreseeability. The person possessing such foresight is expected to so order his conduct that the behavioral tendencies of children are anticipated in a given course of events and provisions made for their safety. Someone has humorously stated that it would help if the teacher were the seventh son of a seventh son, which was the biblical standard for a prophet. Such an approach takes into account the professional insights that a person should gain from having had professional training and experience.

Where a student is exposed to unusual danger the teacher may owe a degree of care or supervision above and beyond that of a normal classroom situation. This is referred to in several decisions as an "extraordinary" duty of care. One such case involved a chemistry teacher where the experiment which was undertaken by the class involved the use of reagents which were explosive in nature. The increased duty of care would probably follow the use of any so-called "dangerous instrumentality." Such activities would probably involve the use of power equipment in a shop, automobiles in driver education, or sharp knives in a unit in vocational agriculture.

The lack of insight in a situation of this kind resulted in a student's death recently. The student was engaged in a dissection experiment in biology in which the teacher allowed the student to take a cat which had been preserved in formaldehyde home with him. He was poisoned by the preservative either by absorption through the skin or breathing an excessive amount of the vaporized material in a poorly ventilated room. The proper role of the teacher should have included careful instructions as to poisonous nature of the preservative and certain safeguards as to its use. Familiarity with certain chemicals sometimes causes us to become careless, and such carelessness frequently results in a charge of negligence.

The prospective teacher often wonders exactly what his duties may be in this area of pupil relations in order to avoid liability. In a recent case, *Morris* v. *Ortiz* (437 P. 2d 652, 1969), the Arizona Supreme Court, in its dissenting opinion, gives an excellent summation of the teacher's responsibility. It reads:

> An examination of the cases and commentaries discloses that three basic duties arise from the teacher-student relationship: (1) the duty to supervise, (2) the duty to exercise good judgment, and (3) the duty to instruct as to correct procedures, particularly (but not exclusively) when potentially hazardous conditions or instrumentalities are present.

The persons practicing in professional education or planning to enter such a career should become familiar with these duties and so structure their professional behaviors to meet such standards.

ARE SCHOOL DISTRICTS ALSO LIABLE FOR PUPIL INJURY?

The common law rule of immunity shields a school district from liability for the negligence of its officers, agents, or employees. Since a school district is an aspect of government, it has been held widely that it should partake of the sovereign immunity. This immunity rule has been modified both judicially and legislatively in a number of states. The highest courts of at least four states have declared that, since sovereign immunity is a judge-made doctrine, the courts have the authority to modify or change the doctrine. The Supreme Court of Illinois was the first to attack the doctrine in the well known case *Molitor* v. *Kaneland Community Unit District No. 302* (163 N.E. 2d 89 1959). The plaintiff was a school child who had been injured when the bus in which he was riding allegedly left the road as a result of the driver's negligence, hit a culvert, and exploded. The child suffered permanent, severe, and painful injuries. The court overturned the "governmental immunity" doctrine, indicating that it felt that this was a carryover of the medieval doctrine of the "King can do no wrong" and was no longer appropriate for a democratic society. Minnesota, Wisconsin, and Arizona courts have also abrogated this doctrine in their states. Other cases in Kentucky, New Jersey, and Pennsylvania have failed in their assaults upon this concept in recent years. However, the immunity for negligent torts does not extend to suits which are filed against the school district for the maintenance of a nuisance.

Liability for various kinds of torts can be established by legislative act. In Texas, the governmental immunity rule was partially abolished by making school districts liable for the negligent acts of employees while using motor-driven vehicles. All other governmental units were stripped of such protection so that institutions of higher education are subject to the various court actions just as a private corporation is liable. A slightly different kind of assault has also made a legislative inroad into sovereign immunity. This kind of act is often called a "safe public places" act. In these statutes, all kinds of governmental bodies are required to keep their facilities which are open to the public in a safe condition. This kind of statute imposes a more onerous burden than a nuisance doctrine because it places a responsibility upon the agency to keep its premises in such condition to prevent injury. In a typical nuisance suit it must be shown that the governmental entity had knowledge of some defect and that nothing had been done to restore it to proper condition through repair or replacement.

Some states have modified the effects of tort litigation against teachers by passing "save harmless" statutes. These acts relieve teachers or school administrators from paying damages adjudged against them in connection with injuries a student sustains from activities within the professional's scope of employment. These statutes generally require the teacher to be named as a defendant but relieve him from paying monetary damages. Professional organizations such as those related to the National Education Association often attempt to assist the teacher in tort litigation by making group liability insurance available as a part of their membership packages. These policies are helpful because they provide fees for legal counsel in addition to the general liability coverage. A statute in Illinois also provides protection for board members, employees, and student teachers. In a recent suit in Illinois (*Treece* v. *Shawnee Community Unit School District*, 233 N.E. 2d 549, 1969) the Supreme Court rejected a plea that such a statute was unconstitutional and refused to permit a school district to gain an indemnification from the teacher whose negligence was associated with the suit.

A TYPICAL LIABILITY SUIT

A case which would adequately illustrate the type of problems arose in a New York school. The physical education teacher had two classmates put on boxing gloves and fight through one round and a part of another. The teacher sat in the bleachers and gave them very little or no supervision. At the conclusion of the partial second round it was evident that one of the students had been injured. His injuries proved to be fatal and the parents brought suit for a recovery of damages against the instructor. The court held for the parents and made a finding of negligence and personal liability. The court said:

> It is the duty of a teacher to exercise reasonable care to prevent injuries. Pupils should be warned before being permitted to engage in a dangerous or hazardous exercise. These young men should have been taught the principles of defense if indeed it was a reasonable thing to permit a slugging match of the kind which the testimony shows this contest to be. The testimony indicates that the teacher failed in his duties in this regard and that he was negligent, and the plaintiff is entitled to recovery. (*LaValley* v. *Stanford*, 70 N.Y.S. 2d 460, 1947.)

It appears that the failure to instruct his student thoroughly in protecting himself against the dangers involved did not meet the foreseeability standard. Perhaps the individual who said that negligence is the study of the mistakes a reasonable man might make was humorously on target.

WHAT CHARACTERISTICS APPEAR MOST COMMONLY IN LIABILITY SUITS?

One of the most common and damaging fact situations in a tort liability situation is that of absence from the place of assigned responsibility. The teacher assumes a responsibility to supervise when a classroom assignment is accepted. When an injury occurs while the teacher is outside the classroom or is not on the playground supervising recess when he or she is supposed to be there provides a very damaging circumstance. This is a difficult situation to remedy entirely because many schools do not have either professional or para-professional personnel available to temporarily release a teacher for emergency errands or simply for restroom breaks. The teacher may be assigned to supervise children from fifteen minutes before class begins in the morning until after they are loaded on school buses after the dismissal bell. Such assignment may include playground supervision during recess and table management during the lunch hour. When a necessary break must be taken from this routine the teacher must often ask a neighbor to look in on his class periodically, use an aide if one is available, or leave the children on their own. None of these solutions is wholly acceptable. This problem could be solved, however, with adequate staffing and a proper communication system.

Another circumstance which frequently arises is that of injury through the use of equipment which has not been kept in repair. Many different kinds of illustrations can be found in various cases. In one recent case a backstop on a baseball field fell on several students. Members of the team which were at bat frequently climbed on the backstop while waiting for their turn at bat. As this practice continued the backstop became more and more wobbly. Finally through repeated use in this fashion it fell. Gymnastic equipment seems especially susceptible to this sort of problem if it were judged by frequency of occurrence.

Shop machinery also becomes suspect because of the incidence of related cases. The story so often sounds like it is repeated again and again. A safety guard on a machine is bent or needs repair. The teacher requisitions the needed repair and it is not immediately forthcoming. The class wants to use the machine on current projects so the teacher removes the guard and permits the students to use the machine. Then an accident occurs which the safety guard was designed to prevent. A simple rule which would prevent most of these injuries would be to refuse to permit a student to use any equipment not in good repair.

Another of the most common charges against teachers in negligence cases is that of inadequate instruction before a pupil attempts some activity where considerable skill is required. A New York case (*Gardner* v. *State*, 22 N.E. 2d 344, 1939) illustrates this problem. The plaintiff was an eleven-year-old girl who brought her suit through a guardian and complained of an injury which occurred in a physical education class. The girl fell while attempting a headstand and fractured a vertebra in her back when she fell. The instructor was blamed for her injury because he had not given proper instruction prior to permitting her to attempt such a stunt. In the brief the instructor was described as being incompetent and called unqualified to teach gymnastics. While there was some question about the quality of the syllabus furnished by the school district, the court concluded that the instructor did not give adequate instruction before permitting the child to attempt the exercise. The appellate court upheld the judgment of the lower court holding, "such a stunt was inherently dangerous to young children." It would appear that such an instructor must be careful to give adequate instruction, permit proper warm-ups, heed student protests concerning lack of confidence, and other skill factors in determining whether to permit the student to perform difficult or dangerous activities. Similar care would be in order where a student was to use power equipment or to undertake to drive behind the wheel in driver education.

WHAT ARE THE DEFENSES AGAINST A NEGLIGENCE CHARGE?

The best defense that any teacher would have in this situation would be a plea that the teacher had acted without negligence or that his professional performance measured up to that expected of a reasonable prudent person in the same or similar circumstances. If the teacher has given adequate instruction in the hazards involved in an activity and has at the same time given proper supervision under the circumstances he may give a positive response to such a charge. A simple denial of negligence may not be enough to satisfy a jury.

Another defense might arise out of a plea of unavoidable accident. This is an appropriate defense where there was nothing that the instructor could have done to prevent the accident. An accident is an event which occurs without fault, carelessness, or omission on the part of the individual involved. Since this is the case, a charge of negligence will usually be defeated by a successful plea of this character. A student's tripping himself by stepping on his own shoestring and falling on an asphalt pavement might be classed as such an event. The teacher or school should not be held to the standard of an insurer of pupil safety where an accident is involved.

The legal doctrine of "assumed risk" also gets lively play in areas of contact sports and often where spectators are injured. A student who decides that he wishes to play football or participate on a wrestling team knows before he joins the team that occasional injuries occur. When he participates with this knowledge he assumes those inherent and obvious risks of the sport. Such a defense is often asserted against a spectator who may be injured by a batted ball in a baseball game. A similar logic is employed. The person who purchases a ticket to a baseball game knows that an occasional foul will be hit into the spectators. Such knowledge generally makes the assumption-of-risk doctrine available in this situation as well as with the participant in the contact sport.

Occasionally a plea of "an act of God" may be available in this kind of situation. Such a circumstance might include a situation where a student was hit by a bolt of lightning where as a member of a student golf team he had taken refuge under a tree during a sudden thunderstorm. This occurrence would have been a direct, immediate, and exclusive operation of the forces of nature. The teacher or coach could make a plea that he could not control or influence such forces and that he was innocent of any casuality and that no amount of foresight would have prevented the injury.

State law differs tremendously as to whether pleas of contributory negligence or comparative negligence would be available to a defendant. Where the injured party failed to exercise the standard of care that he should and such contributory negligence was the proximate cause of the injury, the defendant may use this as a defense. In some states a showing of contributory negligence will result in a judgment for the defendant and has the effect of barring any kind of recovery on the part of the plaintiff. A few states have adopted a comparative negligence statute. Where this concept is utilized, both the plaintiff and defendant may be negligent and, depending upon the extent of the negligence, both parties may be required to pay the damages. Proration of the damages will be decided on a slight, ordinary, or gross basis and the jury makes a determination as to the degree of carelessness of each. On a finding of slight negligence for the defendant the plaintiff may have to bear the major loss in such a case.

SUMMARY

When pre-service teacher trainees read materials such as these in this chapter they become concerned about the risks involved in the teacher's role in dealing with boys and girls in a classroom. Before the student of education becomes too alarmed it should be pointed out that these responsibilities should not be viewed out of perspective. When one considers the hundreds of thousands of transactions which occur daily among teachers, administrators, and children, these incidents which result in litigation are extremely small. The probability of any accident which occurs in the daily professional tasks of the average teacher resulting in a judgment against him is quite small.

The events leading up to litigation in the area of negligent torts do occur every day. No educator can be expected to guarantee that no child in his area of supervision will be injured. The teacher may have taken the most elaborate precautions possible and an accident will still occur. It is helpful to be aware of the exposure to risk in this area and to perform in such a way that it is evident that normal foresight has been exercised and that planning and execution of one's task have been performed as a reasonable and prudent teacher would have performed under the same or similar circumstances. A person who becomes a defendant finds it particularly disconcerting to be confronted with a charge in legal proceedings that he had been negligent in his performance and serious injury to a student has resulted. In addition to the inconvenience and emotional pressures which develop, judgments in other suits which have run as high as four million dollars emphasize the necessity for the teacher to perform as the law requries.

SELECTED BIBLIOGRAPHY

Books

ALEXANDER, KERN, RAY CORNS, and WALTER McCANN. *Public School Law*. St. Paul, Minn.: West Publishing Co., 1969. 734 pages. The authors have treated teacher liability in Chapter 7 in this book of cases and materials on school law. It is well done and the questions utilized at the end of each chapter help to focus the student on the problems of the area which the authors feel are critical.

APPENZELLER, HERB. *From the Gym to the Jury*. Charlottesville, Va.: The Michie Co., 1970. 221 pages. A recent publication devoted to pupil injury in the physical education setting. It is well illustrated and written in a style suitable for pre-service teacher trainees. It would be especially helpful for physical education majors but has excellent sections on several areas which would be helpful to any prospective teacher, for example, supervision.

HAZARD, WILLIAM R. *Education and the Law.* New York: The Free Press, 1971. 480 pages. This author has given an excellent treatment to the tort liability problem both from a school and professional employee point of view. His approach is to give an analysis of the law and then to support it with articles and cases. For the more advanced student in school law the theoretical coverage would not be challenging, but for the student in training it is both interesting and adequate.

NOLTE, M. CHESTER, and JOHN PHILLIP LINN. *School Law for Teachers.* Danville, Ill.: Interstate Printer and Publishers, 1964. 343 pages. This monograph has a good chapter on teacher liability for pupil accident. It would be suitable for any teacher or education student who wishes to have a source which is both readable and technically oriented.

REUTTER, E. EDMUND, JR., and ROBERT R. HAMILTON. *The Law of Public Education.* Mineola, N.Y.: The Foundation Press, 1970. 654 pages. The treatment given to tort liability in this text would be one more suited to a student of school administration. It includes in its discussion the liability of a school district as well as its employees and provides a perspective for a school administrator.

SARNER, HARVEY. *The Nurse and the Law.* Philadelphia: W. B. Saunders, 1968. This treatise is one of several written recently directed toward persons who have professional careers ahead in nursing. Every school nurse should read Chapter 4, which deals with the problems of negligence from their point of responsibility.

Periodicals and Paperbacks

BOLMEIER, E. C. "Trends in Pupil Transportation Litigation. " *School Board Journal.* February 1960. Pp. 38-40. An article which gives some background on the increasing problem of liability for pupil injury in the area of school bus operation. The author provides several trend analyses which have since happened.

PETERSON, LEROY J. *Yearbook of School Law, 1972.* Topeka, Kan.: National Organization on Legal Problems in Education, 1972. 260 pages. The N.O.L.P.E. issues an annual yearbook which has a chapter devoted to the problems associated with pupil injury. In this volume, Chapter 2 is devoted to an excellent analysis of both doctrinal positions and case law.

Research Division, National Education Association. *The Teacher's Day in Court: Review of 1970.* Washington, D.C.: National Education Association, 1971. 79 pages. Each year a compilation of this kind is published by the Research Division concerning litigation which has involved teachers. A regular section of the report is on Liability for Pupil Injury.

SEITZ, REYNOLDS C. "Legal Responsibility under Tort Law of School Personnel and School Districts as Regards Negligent Conduct Toward

Pupils." 45 *Hastings Law Journal* 495 (May 1964). A well written law review article which includes a section of importance on the duty to supervise. The author treats with conservative viewpoints the problems associated with student teachers and other non-certified personnel.

STRAHAN, RICHARD D. *Legal Briefs for School Administrators.* Houston, Texas: Bureau of Education Research and Services, University of Houston, 1971. 120 pages. Briefs 7, 8, and 9 in this series are devoted to liability for pupil injury. The briefs are written in an easy-to-understand question-and-answer style that is designed for school boards and administrators.

CHAPTER 10

Professional Negotiations

One of the most controversial movements in education during this century has been the attempt by teachers to gain the right to participate more actively in the decision-making process in American public education. It has been augmented to a great degree by the intense rivalry that has been evident between the giants in the field of teacher organizations. Until recently the American Federation of Teachers was a minimal-impact organization. When the A.F.T. won the representation rights for the New York City teachers' organization, a new milestone was reached. Its aggressive style of teacher representation appealed greatly to teachers in many of the major metropolitan areas. In many of these schools expenditures were low and "blackboard jungle" conditions had been tolerated a long time. The brick and glass canyons were to become the battleground for teacher loyalties.

The National Education Association and its state and local affiliates have long been the spokesmen for the majority of American educators. It had majored for many years in a conservative, highly stylized representation through which it drew the support of most of the professional educators. The backbone of its organization became the state affiliates, which were made up of both teachers and administrators in their memberships. In local schools it was often the pressure of an interested superintendent who gained 100 percent membership in the local, state, and national levels of the organization. Membership of administrators in teachers' organizations has been one of the major issues in the attempt to maintain their preeminent position in teacher loyalties. The N.E.A. continues to dominate the medium- and small-city scene but is engaged in a nationwide struggle to maintain its strength. This epic struggle for support among the nation's classroom teachers has fostered an activist role for both organizations. A number of educational leaders have gone on record as favoring a merger of the N.E.A. and A.F.T. into a single organization of teachers.

An understanding of the forces which are now at work in public education can be gained by looking at collective activities in the private sector of our economy. It would appear that the forces which shaped the labor movement almost a century ago are appearing in the organizational efforts being expended in connection with teachers and other public employees in governmental service. In the nature of social forces, management could not forever control the destinies and daily lives of those who labored in mine and factory. Some degree of parity in the operation of the private segment of the economy was gained through distribution of power to working groups through collective activities. A short historical narrative will contribute some understandings to the prospective teacher in regard to these activities. The beginning teacher in today's schools should be prepared to make an intelligent decision as to the role that he or she will take in regard to both joining and participating in professional organizations.

COLLECTIVE ACTIVITIES IN THE PRIVATE SECTOR

Employees in the private sector of the nation's economy initiated efforts at employee organization and concerted actions around the middle of the nineteenth century. Because of the harsh laws governing group activities and the criminal penalties which were often imposed, the first labor unions were organized as secret societies of workingmen. Management was unfettered in its use of economic power and the wealth generated by a few through the use of sweat-shop conditions and substandard wages is now legendary. The imbalance created by such conditions and the exploitation made possible through them fueled the beginnings of the labor movement.

The advocates of collective activities among workingmen made slow headway during the last quarter of the nineteenth century. It is estimated that it took Uriah Stephens and the Knights of Labor at least a decade to enlist its first 20,000 members. These first efforts at organization spawned a peculiar grouping of philosophies. Some were tinged with Marxism and argued that the entire system should be abolished and replaced with some other means of benefits distribution besides wages. All stressed that the workingmen had some kind of basic right to participate more fully in the economic benefits generated through their labors.

The ruthless use of economic power through layoffs during economic slowdowns and the capricious use of authority in discharging those classed as troublemakers by management brought more determined effort on the part of union organizers. The notion that the worker should have some right to participate in decisions regarding wages and working conditions grew steadily. The individual worker soon concluded that freedom of contract between unequals does not create equality in bargaining. As the groups grew more sophisticated, group activities such as the boycott were used. In a short while it became one of the most powerful weapons available to labor groups.

Early in the labor-management struggle, management groups relied heavily upon legislative action and judicial intervention. In both England and America prosecutions were often attempted under the crime of conspiracy where attempts were made to organize collective labor action. In an English case, *Commonwealth* v. *Hunt* (4 Metcalf 111, 1842), the court went on record as refusing to grant a decision which would permit criminal prosecution of striking employees. As public sentiment shifted away from the use of criminal prosecution, management then became reliant upon judicial intervention through the use of injunctions. These writs were utilized when the court found that these conditions existed either individually or severally: (1) criminal conspiracy, (2) violence or threatened violence, (3) encouraging or enticing employees in breach of contracts, and (4) private nuisance defined as interference with private business rights. Numerous court decisions upheld the right of capital to combine but continued to enforce a doctrine that combination or conspiracy for bettering labor conditions was unlawful. After the violence and destruction that marked the Pullman Strike, public sentiment toward labor's right to organize began to change.

The public interest in the employee's right to organize and to deal with his employer about working conditions found expression in legislation such as the Erdman Act (1898) and the Clayton Act (1914). When the narrow judicial interpretation of the Clayton Act in the *Duplex Printing Press Co.* v. *Deering* case (254 U.S. 443, 1921) permitted the continued use of injunctive orders, Congress responded by passing the Norris-LaGuardia Act (1932). Through these acts the use of injunctions to halt strikes, picketing, holding mass meetings, advertising, and other collective actions was no longer permitted, barring violence or fraud. Special administrative bodies were established to provide for the adjustment and settling of labor disputes and the federal courts were made available to enforce labor agreements and legislation. As a result many of the prerogatives which were once considered the domain of management are subject to discussion and negotiation. Collective bargaining has become the method by which labor participates in the decision-making process and through which some parity of power distribution has occurred.

COLLECTIVE ACTIVITIES IN PUBLIC EDUCATION

The origins of formal collective negotiations in education are of more recent nature. They began shortly after the turn of the century while labor in the private sector of the economy was winning public support and legislation to enable it to bargain from a more equitable position. Teachers were not as successful in gaining public sentiment. When the teachers in Chicago sought to join an organization called the Chicago Federation of Teachers in 1917, they lost their jobs. The Chicago Board of Education passed a resolution which prohibited membership in a teachers' union. When teachers violated the rule, they were dismissed. The court, upholding the dismissals, stated: "Union membership was inimical to proper discipline, prejudicial to the efficiency of the teaching force, and detrimental to the welfare of the public school system." (People ex rel. *Fursman* v. *City of Chicago*, 116 N.E. 158, 1917.) As late as 1930 the Seattle public schools had a policy which stated that their teachers could not join the American Federation of Labor or its locals. In the case *Seattle High School Chapter No. 200, A.F.T.* v. *Sharples* (293 P. 999, 1930), the court turned down a Fourteenth Amendment plea when it said "Refusal to employ anyone is not a denial of a constitutional right to follow his chosen profession."

Two decades would pass before the right to organize and collectively bargain would be available to educators. In a 1951 case, *Norwalk Teachers Association* v. *Board of Education of the City of Norwalk* (83 A. 2d 482, 1951), a Connecticut court permitted a teachers' organization to organize for the purpose of demanding and receiving recognition for collective bargaining. The right to so organize was conditioned upon the organization's willingness to forego the strike threat. Subsequent events have assured most public employees the right to organize and negotiate from a collective or concerted position. Since the 1961 law passed in Wisconsin guaranteeing public employees the right to organize and bargain collectively, numerous other states have passed laws permitting teachers and other public employees to organize and to bargain in regard to wages and working conditions.

More recent court cases such as *McLaughlin* v. *Telindis* (398 F. 2d 287, 1968) conclude that the First Amendment to the federal Constitution confers the right to form and join a labor union in a case where teachers had been dismissed for union activity. In most states bargainable issues generally are limited to wages, hours, and working conditions but may also include issues related to textbooks, curriculum, in-service training, student teaching programs, personnel hiring and assignment practices, leaves of absence, and non-instructional duties. The tempo of organizational activity has been greatly increased. Although most state statutes prohibit strikes by public employees, the incidence of such activities has greatly accelerated. Teacher strikes in Philadelphia and other cities have resulted in organizational leaders being jailed on contempt of court charges when injunctions ordering teachers back to work in the classroom were ignored. There seems to be little reason for use of such legal weapons when public health or safety is not at stake. Excessive use of such tactics may very well provide greater public support for the causes which the teachers are attempting to further.

In a number of states legislation in the professional negotiation area has provided only consultation statutes. Such a statute was passed in Texas in 1967, and was incorporated into the Texas Education Code, Section 13.901. The statute reads:

> Section 13.901 Employment Consultation with Teachers
> The Board of Trustees of each independent school district, rural high school district, and common school district, and their administrative personnel, may consult with teachers with respect to matters of educational policy and conditions of employment; and such boards of trustees may adopt and make reasonable rules, regulations and agreements to provide for such consultation. This section shall not limit or affect the power of said trustees to manage and govern said schools.

Many teacher organizations have taken advantage of this type of statute to organize and enter into consultation over wages and working conditions. The impact of agreements which are negotiated is greatly limited by the fact that they are not legally binding. Another section of Texas law, Vernon's Annotated Texas Statutes, Article 5154 (c), forbids collective bargaining contracts between officers of municipal subdivisions of the state and organizations representing public employees.

The statute does permit representation by an employee group in behalf of a grievance arising from a condition of an individual's employment contract so long as the organization does not contend that it has a right to strike. In a style somewhat reminiscent of the conspiracy laws against private sector concerted activity, this statute declares all kinds of group activity in the public employee sector to be against public policy. It does preserve the right of the individual to quit his job so long as the action is not a part of a concerted work stoppage. This statute was followed up in the Texas Education Code, Section 13.216, with a statutory section which provides that the State Commissioner of Education shall suspend any teacher who violates the provisions of the previously mentioned act.

THE NATURE OF THE NEGOTIATION PROCESS

The negotiation or bargaining process has been greatly impeded by several arguments which have been put forward that the public employer-teacher relationship is fundamentally different from employer-employee relationship in the private sector of the economy. The heart of the argument revolves around the nature of school board authority. It is said to be a delegated authority associated with contractual fixing of conditions of work in the public service and that this authority cannot be delegated to another party. From this point of view any limitation on the authority to change conditions of employment is a serious invasion of school board authority. In states where this viewpoint prevails the final decisional authority has been left with the board of education without any necessity for resolving any breakdown in the negotiating process.

The negotiation process begins with statutory authority which enables a teacher or employee group to organize and be represented before the school board to discuss wages, hours, and conditions of employment. The process is begun in the typical statute by the employee group organizing, and when a majority of the employees of a given classification are members, the organization calls for a representation election. If a majority of the employees within a classification vote for a particular organization, it is designated as the negotiating unit for that class of employees. Whether the organization may be the sole representative for a class of employees and have other privileges such as dues check-offs, representation fees for non-members, use of school facilities, and use of in-house mailing procedures will depend upon the particular state statute or local school board policy. When both the employee organization and the school board have chosen their representatives the process is ready to begin.

The employee organization usually takes the initiative in the negotiating process by putting a group of proposals or concerns before the board team. The United States Supreme Court in *N.L.R.B.* v. *Wooster Div. of Borg-Warner Corp.* (356 U.S. 342, 1958) established or recognized three categories of proposals which might come before the employer:

1. Those that are illegal and therefore cannot be bargained about.
2. Those that may be bargained about if the parties voluntarily wish to do so.
3. Those that are mandatory and must be bargained about.

These positions would not necessarily be binding upon a school board, in that they are an interpretation of the National Labor Relations Act, but many of the guidelines used in the negotiations process have been drawn from the private sector's experience. Wages, hours, and working conditions normally fall in the mandatory negotiations area and are the areas often mentioned in professional negotiation statutes. Many of the normal concerns of teachers also fall in this area, such as: class size, holidays, in-service training, supervision of playgrounds, duty-free lunch periods, planning time, and club sponsorships. Many of the items which are often called administrative prerogatives may also be negotiated if the school board wishes to consider them. These would include items such as: teacher assignment, teacher evaluation, processing of payrolls, recruiting and selection of administrators or teachers, and school calendars. The process is expected to be a proposal-counter proposal with each party taking an active role until agreement is reached or an impasse results.

Where the employer is a public employer there is less compulsion to reach an agreement than in the private sector. The teacher organization does not have the devices or procedures to compel agreement where all management decisions are left in the hands of school boards without any requirement to mediate, arbitrate, or submit to some government employees relations boards, and the employee is forbidden to strike. Early in the negotiations process between school boards and teacher organizations the bargaining tended to break down into a teacher demand-board capitulation situation. Teacher groups borrowed very readily from labor bargaining tactics and training. Boards often used as their agents school administrators who had little background in bargaining techniques. Their response to teacher demands was often compromises which were in effect concessions to the employee position.

It is significant to note that a school board cannot be compelled to negotiate things which are illegal. Many of the relationships which exist between teachers and school boards are controlled directly by state law. It would be fruitless to bargain about an agency shop if state statutes forbid any type of closed shop arrangement. Demands in regard to minimum salary schedules, retirement benefits, required curricula, and other characteristics of the public education program which are directly controlled by statute would similarly be futile. Most authorities in the labor relations field suggest that the school board move cautiously and responsibly when it moves into the area which it declares to be an administrative or management prerogative about which it will not negotiate. It is especially frustrating to employees to find that they have legitimate suggestions or interests in a particular aspect of school operation only to find that the board takes the position that such aspects of the program are non-negotiable.

Since the strike is prohibited to most public employees, the means available to employee organizations to resolve deadlocks in the negotiations process are most important. Perhaps the Wisconsin statute is one of those that spells out the procedures with the best ground rules (Wisconsin Statutes Ann., Section 111.70). In its procedure the Wisconsin Employment Relations Board is empowered to appoint a fact-finder to investigate deadlocked negotiations and make written findings and recommendations which are to be made public. Although he has no power to enforce his findings, promulgation of them to the public often enlists enough public interest and support to bring about a solution.

The purpose of the entire process is to bring about an agreement between the employer-employee groups to produce maximal educational benefits to the children of the district. Most statutes in this area require the agreements to be reduced to writing and the agreement becomes the operating guidelines for the district's teachers and administrators. The usual time limitations upon such group agreement is usually one year, though many include provisions that in a circumstance where agreement does not occur that the current agreement should remain in force until such time as a new agreement is reached.

SHOULD TEACHERS STRIKE?

Teachers often ask themselves how they can bring about or exert pressure on school boards to accept various proposals that they wish to accomplish at the bargaining table. Some who take an activist position advocate the use of all kinds of activity which will exert maximum pressure on the school board to accomplish their objectives. Numerous teacher groups have said they will strike whether or not the statute permits it. Others say that teachers should organize picket lines and march to demonstrate their determination to attain contract goals. Another approach is to impose sanctions upon a district by having teachers return contracts unsigned and to discourage others from coming into the district by circulating adverse publicity. Without attempting to evaluate entirely the advantages or disadvantages of such organizational postures, one should point out that teachers are still dealing with impressionable minds and are still in the position of filling an exemplary profession. It appears that the effect of the strike or the picket line is to use children as their weapon. Teachers can hardly permit themselves to become object lessons in how to violate the law.

OBSERVATIONS OF THE NEGOTIATION PROCESS

Careful observation of the negotiation process between teacher organizations and school boards indicates that persons who plan certain careers in education should be aware of the developments in the area of their planned professional involvement. One thing stands out in this process. The crux of the majority of teacher grievances and proposals which are offered at the bargaining table is the relationship that the teachers have with a unit administrator, who generally carries the title of building principal. The building principal carries the responsibility of providing instructional leadership and unit management for the ongoing of the instructional program. He represents the initial level of administrative leadership in the school district and is responsible for relationships with most of the school's clientele. Most of the human relations problems of the school focus on this particular office whether they are generated by contacts with pupils, teachers, parents, superiors, or the school board. As one principal expressed it, "this is where the nitty-gritty happens."

As a consequence most of the proposals submitted to the school board revolve around the teacher-principal relationship. Often the middle administrators are not on the negotiating team and concessions are often made without consideration of the effect of the capitulation on the role and expectations of the principal. Many principals now feel that their primary responsibilities are now to open and close their buildings and to administer the Master Agreement between the school board and the teachers' organization. The principals' organizations across the country have responded by attempting to get legislation passed which defines their administrative role. A model code provision which is recommended by the National Association of Secondary School Principals is available for this purpose. The strategy behind this move was to put the school board's representative in the position of being able to say that certain areas of school operation are established by law to be the duties of principals and thus cannot be a subject of negotiations. Several states have already adopted such laws.

It would certainly be prudent at this point to suggest to aspiring school administrators that they carefully assess their own personalities to determine whether or not they are emotionally and personally suited to such an area of potential conflict. If they do not possess and maintain an emotional makeup which is capable of tolerating a certain amount of turbulence the principalship may not at all be desirable as a career objective. Many of the concerns now expressed about principals may be nothing more than the fact that they are the local representative of the establishment. The result is that much of the teacher and pupil activism may be directed at them in their representative role rather than in their personal role. The quality of administrative leadership which they offer may not be an issue at all. When this sort of thing happens the administrator must be capable of absorbing the emotional impact associated with confrontation without permitting it to destroy him.

SUMMARY

It goes without saying more that the school board-employee organization bargaining situation will probably not only continue but will tend to accelerate. The issues which are constantly raised by administrators and board members to the effect that collective actions will undermine school board authority will not be sufficient to stem the tide of events which flow in this direction. Almost without exception the state legislatures as they convene are confronted each session with a new barrage of bills which either create the right to collectively bargain or expand rights which are already established. There are some concerns with this process toward which some remarks are pertinent.

Individuals who are entering the profession should be well aware of the process which will more likely than not spell out the conditions under which they will serve in the classroom. They should participate actively in the process. Individuals who do not represent the professional sentiments of the membership should not be permitted to get in control of the teachers' organization. The organization input into the bargaining or negotiating process will be no better than the quality of the teachers' own concerns. The model of the private sector of the economy is not appropriate for educational organizations. There are goals in dealing with children which are held in common with administrative groups, parents, and school boards. There are many settings in which the adversary posture must be laid aside while organizational momentum is developed toward goal accomplishment.

School boards should likewise drop their effort in maintaining legal prescriptions of the bargaining process in the public sector. Greater interest should be developed in meeting the legitimate concerns of teachers involved in the process. They too should search for models to be used in the public sector which expeditiously solve the procedural and other problems such as staffing, budget, and public acceptance. Just as private management has developed means of coping with this type of procedure, the school board can also successfully develop new modes of behavior in working with teacher and pupil groups. The trends of court decisions in regard to teacher and pupil rights is not likely to change, so a school management style must be developed which will utilize the process for the improvement of the educational program.

The transition period can be either facilitative or resistive, dependent upon the quality of educational statesmanship provided by the nation's administrators. The old symbols of authority are largely gone. New styles of administration must emerge. The paternalism so long reflected in authoritarian styles of administrative practices seems to be anachronistic in today's setting. Tomorrow's needs require an administrative style which can accommodate desires for participatory roles for pupils and teachers and yet move the organization toward its desired goals.

SELECTED BIBLIOGRAPHY

Books

CARLTON, PATRICK W., and HAROLD I. GOODWIN. *The Collective Dilemma: Negotiations in Education.* Worthington, Ohio: Charles A. Jones Publishing Co., 1969. 339 pages. A collection of readings which are well chosen to attempt to convey some of the issues as related to attitudes and behaviors on the part of the participants. Perhaps a little oriented to the pessimistic view, but timely.

DRURY, ROBERT L. *Law and the School Superintendent.* Cincinnati: W. H. Anderson Co., 1958. 339 pages. One of the early texts which suggest a role for the superintendent of schools in the bargaining process. In Section 2.10 the author outlines with some degree of accuracy the role the teachers' organizations would likely expect him to play.

ELAM, STANLEY M., MYRON LIEBERMAN, and MICHAEL H. MOSKOW. *Readings on Collective Negotiations in Public Education.* Chicago: Rand McNally, 1967. 470 pages. An extensive book of readings for the person generating an interest in collective negotiations for the first time. Special emphasis is put on articles which have historical significance and viewpoints from various organizations representing teachers and administrators at both the public school and college levels.

National Organization on Legal Problems in Education. *Critical Issues in School Law.* Topeka, Kan.: National Organization on Legal Problems in Education, 1970. 199 pages. The first article in this publication is one entitled "The Analysis of a Strike," which is a description of the strike which occurred in the Los Angeles, California, schools. Of particular interest is that segment of the article which develops a strike plan which gives tremendous insight into problems of keeping schools open during a teacher strike.

PERRY, CHARLES R., and WESLEY A. WILDMAN. *The Impact of Negotiations in Public Education: The Evidence from the Schools.* Worthington, Ohio: Charles A. Jones Publishing Co., 1970. 254 pages. The authors in this volume emphasize the practices involved in negotiation and the impact that they have had on public education. It offers sound analysis of the dynamics of the process and newer insights into the roles of administrators, board members, and teachers.

PETERSON, LEROY J., RICHARD A. ROSSMILLER, and MARLIN M. VOLZ. *The Law and Public School Operation.* New York: Harper & Row, 1969. 579 pages. There is a short but well documented section in this text on professional negotiations. It provides an excellent insight into both private and public sources which have influenced the course of acceptance of public employee negotiations.

REUTTER, E. EDMUND, JR., and ROBERT R. HAMILTON. *The Law of Public Education.* Mineola, N.Y.: The Foundation Press, 1970. 654 pages. The authors in this text treat professional negotiations in a wider text of terms and conditions of employment of teachers. Holidays, strikes, sanctions, and other techniques used by teachers are discussed in their legal settings.

SHILS, EDWARD B., and C. TAYLOR WHITTIER. *Teachers, Administrators, and Collective Bargaining.* New York: Thomas Y. Crowell, 1968. 580 pages.

A text which highlights the beginnings of teacher negotiating and the crucial steps in preparing for and conducting negotiating sessions. It is more procedurally oriented rather than legal or technical.

Periodicals and Pamphlets

ACKERLY, ROBERT L., and W. STANFIELD JOHNSON. *Critical Issues in Negotiations Legislation.* Washington, D.C.: National Association of Secondary School Principals, 1969. 35 pages. Another of the Professional Negotiations Pamphlets; it is directed toward an understanding of the legislation associated with negotiations and its improvement. It should be required reading of any person who works with a professional legislation committee.

American School Board Journal. *Bargaining for Beginners.* Evanston, Ill.: National School Boards Association, 1969. 22 pages. A pamphlet designed to acquaint school board members with the bargaining process and to help them design strategies for use in meeting and successfully bargaining with teachers.

EPSTEIN, BENJAMIN. *What Is Negotiable?* Washington, D.C.: National Association of Secondary School Principals, 1969. 28 pages. A short and easily read pamphlet in which the author discusses the issues which should and should not become issues for negotiation. It is written in professional language that any teacher or education student should understand.

SCHMIDT, CHARLES T., JR., HYMAN PARKER, and BOB REPAS. *A Guide to Collective Negotiations in Education.* East Lansing, Mich.: Michigan State University, 1967. 85 pages. This publication has two sections which are especially worth reading which deal with the Michigan statutes dealing with teacher negotiation and one on grievance procedures which are worth consideration for those seriously interested in the process.

SEITZ, REYNOLD C. "Legal Aspects of Public School Teacher Negotiating and Participating in Concerted Activities." 49 *Marquette Law Review* 487. 1965-66. A most perceptive treatment of many of the legal issues involving teacher negotiations. This article is especially helpful in terms of understanding constitutional and other issues raised by teacher demands, such as exclusive representation and others.

Afterword

Other significant issues could have been treated in a book dealing with the influence of court decisions on the operation of public schools in the United States. The concepts which have been discussed in the text are designed to give insights into areas where the college student who is engaged in a pre-service program in teacher education is not likely to gain many knowledges. School law courses are normally taught in graduate-level programs so that the beginning teacher goes into supervised student teaching and is inducted into the profession with few ideas as to what the court decisions are about or how they should influence practices in the public school classroom. Many areas could only be given surface treatment in chapters as short as these chapters had to be. Additional information can be gained by following through and considering information given in the recommended Bibliographies.

A person entering the teaching professional area during this era will find a changed climate awaiting him. It is essential that he know his contract and personal rights. He must also realize that he will be held to a higher standard of personal performance and knowledge. Procedures to establish individual accountability are being tested over the country, and these will heighten the stresses placed upon the individuals engaged in teaching. Professional organizations will be needed both to insure individual growth and to provide the support needed while adapting to the demands of a given situation. Creative effort will be needed to translate court decisions into operational programs which meet judicial and constitutional standards. New educational goals which meet the needs of a multicultural society and a new ethic which will meet the broadened standards of "due process" and "equal protection" are intellectual as well as operational challenges. Education in our society has many new frontiers for those who are intellectually, emotionally, and legally prepared for them.